TROUBLE SONGS

BEFORE YOU START TO READ THIS BOOK, take this moment to think about making a donation to punctum books, an independent non-profit press,
@ https://punctumbooks.com/support/
If you're reading the e-book, you can click on the image below to go directly to our donations site. Any amount, no matter the size, is appreciated and will help us to keep our ship of fools afloat. Contributions from dedicated readers will also help us to keep our commons open and to cultivate new work that can't find a welcoming port elsewhere. Our adventure is not possible without your support.
Vive la open-access.

Fig. 1. Hieronymus Bosch, *Ship of Fools* (1490–1500)

TROUBLE SONGS. Copyright © 2018 by Jeff T. Johnson. This work carries a Creative Commons BY-NC-SA 4.0 International license, which means that you are free to copy and redistribute the material in any medium or format, and you may also remix, transform and build upon the material, as long as you clearly attribute the work to the authors (but not in a way that suggests the authors or punctum books endorses you and your work), you do not use this work for commercial gain in any form whatsoever, and that for any remixing and transformation, you distribute your rebuild under the same license. http://creativecommons.org/licenses/by-nc-sa/4.0/

First published in 2018 by punctum books, Earth, Milky Way.
https://punctumbooks.com

ISBN-13: 978-1-947447-44-8 (print)
ISBN-13: 978-1-947447-45-5 (ePDF)

LCCN: 2018930421
Library of Congress Cataloging Data is available from the Library of Congress

Book design: Vincent W.J. van Gerven Oei
Cover image: Philippe de Champaigne, *Still-Life With a Skull* (ca. 1671).

HIC SVNT MONSTRA

TROUBLE SONGS
A Musicological Poetics

Jeff T. Johnson

for Josephine K. Few

Track List

Part One
I Must Be the Devil's Daughter   15

"Country Blues," Dock Boggs	17
Trouble Songs: An Invocation	19
David Lynch, Trouble Man	23
Trouble Forms: Structure & Approach	25
Modes of Trouble — Terms — Elaboration, Embellishment, Embodiment	27
Not Wanting to (Formally) Listen to Trouble Songs	33
History	35
Trouble Song as Speech Act & Magic Language	38
Genre Trouble	42
I'm New Here: The Trouble With Covers	45
The Incantation of Trouble	47
Trouble Is a Lonesome Town, Lee Hazlewood	48
History, Continued	49
"Trouble" vs. "Remember"	50
"Troubled Waters," Cat Power	51
"Paths of Victory," Cat Power	52
Discomfort & the Cover Condition	53
"Good Intentions Paving Company," Joanna Newsom	54
Trouble in Dreams, Destroyer	55

***

Part Two
I Know a Place Where There's Still Something Going On   59

"Trouble" Songs	61
"Summer Days," Bob Dylan	63
You Know That I'm No Good — Amy Winehouse & the Trouble Barrier	64
Trouble With History	66
"You Can't Put Your Arms Around a Memory"	68
The Secret Rider	69
Not Wanting to Listen to Trouble Songs, Refrain	71
The Trouble With Superman	73
Trouble Returns	76
Lost in the Paradise	78
Enter Trouble America	80
Fugue on Anthology Minor	81
Occupied	85
We Who Are [in] Trouble	87
We Recruit(ed), We Reinscribe(d)	88
*NYT*rouble, World Trouble (Hidden Tracks)	89

***

Part Three
Trouble on the Line   91

Take Apart: Room by Room	93
Annie Clark, Becoming "Kerosene"	94
If I Stay Here, Trouble Will Find Me	96
Trouble Will Find You	100
XXII: Trouble on the Line	102
One Kind Favor ("See That My Grave Is Kept Clean")	107
Down the Line	109
Trouble in Heart	111
The Circle	112
I'm a Fool to Want You	116

Lay It Down	118
Cause You're Mine	121

***

Part Four
Back in Trouble   123

Return to Trouble, That Lonesome Town	125
Death's Head, Proud Flesh	128
Nobody Here but We in Trouble	130
A Whole House	132
Nobody Knows (Great Things to Small)	133
Catch a Fire: One Thing for Another	140
By Any Other Name ("Trouble, Heartaches & Sadness")	141
Notes	143
The Author Role	146
The Champ	147
Dear Trouble	150
The End of Trouble	151
Song	152
Last Call	153

***

Appendices   157

Appendix A: Demo	159
Appendix B: Cover	163
Appendix C: Remix	168
Works Cited	179
Index of Names	185
Index of Titles	191
Credits	199

Part One

I MUST BE THE DEVIL'S DAUGHTER

"Country Blues," Dock Boggs[1]

Come all you good time people[2] is the only way it starts. The banjo may have been playing forever — waiting for the singer to arrive, or indifferent to his presence — : a stage. Or the singer is the instrument of the (infernal) banjo.[3] Still, it is impossible to decide whether the voice or the banjo comes first, though *both* does not seem to be an option. The dynamics are too irregular, too separate, for simultaneity. The third instrument, recording static, holds them together.[4]

One or the other, the voice or the banjo, might be in a different world. Or they are not in the world together, or they are each in a world that is not this one — three worlds.

Forty dollars won't pay my fine. The song goes around and around, insisting that it play all night (for it is always night in the song, always night when the song plays, though the song is always playing — the song doesn't stop; we stop listening to it). Money can't reach it, and we can't believe the singer can reach heaven, though he sings to us from the afterworld, where corn whiskey and pretty women surround him, *sweet heaven when I die.* Meanwhile, before or after, *pretty women is a-troublin my mind.* He's in a prison cell, he's in a hole in the ground, dead drunk and buried by us good people, (he's) grinning his empty grin at us. It shines through the soil we throw on his face.

---

1   This cover is influenced by versions and visions of Boggs by Greil Marcus, particularly in *Invisible Republic* (1997) and his "Old Weird America" course at The New School.
2   transcription fails delivery: *pee-ee-ee-ee-puuuuull…*
3   Lee Smith's *The Devil's Dream* presents Satan's laughter as music, played by and playing the players of the song.
4   See/hear Lou Reed's version of Blind Lemon Jefferson's "See That My Grave Is Kept Clean," in which Reed plays (on guitar) the recording static from Jefferson's 1928 record, as collected on volume three of Harry Smith's *Anthology of American Folk Music* (1952). Reed's revisitation appears on *The Harry Smith Project: Anthology of American Folk Music Revisited Vol. 2* (2006).

When I'm dead and buried / My pale face turned to the sun…

The singer calls us around while he has plenty of money. As long as his pockets are full, we drink along. When the money's gone, so are we. He's gone too, all alone with a woman drinking to his memory:

> *Last time I seen my little woman[,]⁵ good people,*
> *She had a wine glass in her hand,*
> *She was drinking down her troubles*
> *With a low-down sorry man.*

Her trouble is a man, and she's drinking with a trouble man,⁶ and she's drinking her troubles, and he watches her as he de-materializes. She joins the invisible chorus of betrayal, along with a woman who promises to bail the singer out of jail, but never gets around to it before she leaves the song. We, good people, join the chorus as we leave, and we can never leave, and our voices dry up in our throats. Boggs too is both here and not here, as we are there and not there.

If I don't quit my rowdy ways / have trouble at my door. There it is now, Boggs's fingernails scratching the banjo's face, digging at the dirt scattered there. *If I'd a-listened to my momma[,] good people / I wouldn't a-been here today.* Wherever he is, we can find him in the soil of the song, that too-shallow grave we pass right through if we don't watch our step. If we do (watch our step), that death's head keeps nodding away at us. *Come all you good time people…*

---

5   the comma makes sense, but Boggs eschews (or transcends) the comma.
6   *Got me singing yeah!* as Marvin Gaye had it ("Trouble Man").

Trouble Songs: An Invocation

> *But before long, the words lost their sense completely, becoming little more than a means to regulate breath — which, she soon supposed, was as good a use for them as any.*
> — Ted Mooney, *The Same River Twice*

> *Denaturalization of one's personal and cultural premise.*
> — Caroline Bergvall, "Middling English"

> *Trouble, trouble, I've had it all my days / It seems like trouble going to follow me to my grave*
> — Bessie Smith, "Downhearted Blues"

Language is not only a means for saying, language is what we are saying. *Record,* we say, and we mean album, or we mean vinyl, or we mean history. Let the record show.[7] That we say record and not CD, tape, album or document is integral to what we are saying. We place ourselves in history, and we place history in ourselves when we use particular language.[8]

History exists as Trouble Song and is troubled by its[9] representation. Distinctions between Trouble Songs collapse into versions, iterations, variations and interpretations. Just so, trouble is inescapable, and can be only partially elaborated. To speak the word "trouble" is to invoke trouble. The Trouble Songs project is

---

7   that we were there.
8   Speaking of "the dispersed, intensely regional transformations" of English as it is used and altered over time, Caroline Bergvall reports: "This transport flows across both diachronic and synchronic routes, sheds as much as it drags historical account along with itself" (14). The term *diachronic* refers, in linguistic study, to "the historical development of a language," while *synchronic* refers to a descriptive approach to the state of language at a given time (*Oxford English Dictionary* online). Trouble Songs, as a study, explores the continuum between these approaches, which makes it essentially diachronic in scope, though there will be moments of synchronic reflection, particularly within the moment of song. To return to and reiterate Bergvall, "This transport flows across both."
9   Call it "History, Trouble Song."

such an invocation and elaboration. When we say "trouble," we refer to the history of trouble whether or not we have it in mind. When we sing trouble, we sing (with) history. We sing history here; we summon trouble.

A Trouble Song is a complaint, a grievance, an aside, a come-on, a confession, an admission, a resignation, a plea. It's an invitation — to sorrow, frustration, darkness. It's part of a conversation, or it's a soliloquy, and it's often an apostrophe. The listener overhears the song, with sympathy. The song is meant for someone else, someone dead or gone. The singer doesn't care who hears, and the song is a dare. Or it's a false wager — to speak trouble is to summon trouble, but it's already here.

Trouble is loss — or the threat of loss, which is the appearance of loss. A Trouble Song is impossible speech; it speaks about the inability to speak. Trouble is a lack of what once was possessed, a desire in absence, an absence in desire. Trouble is the presence of absence, a present of loss. It is impotence and despair, but a Trouble Song is not a negation or a denial. Its admission is its invitation. Trouble is spoken not only in resignation and exasperation, but in defiance. Trouble is spoken as a challenge to death and defeat. In a Trouble Song, there is history, but there is no past — trouble is here and now. Which is to say, there is history, but it is not (the) past.

Trouble has a cousin: problem. They are related, but not by blood. *The problem* can be articulated, while *trouble* doesn't need an article, slips away from the most slippery terms, escapes parts of speech, without leaving us. "Trouble" is the signifier that refuses to signify, or will only call itself. Trouble is its own copula.[10] When we sing trouble, we are inextricable with it — and in-

---

10 To say *She troubles me,* or *She is trouble* — or "She was trouble," as private dick Philip Marlowe, via Raymond Chandler, says in *The Big Sleep* (17) — is to bind two things that were different, but have become inseparable. Untie them, and they are still linked. To be in trouble is to be. (Copula is etymologically linked with couple and copulate; all of these forms are intimately linked with trouble.)

deed we sing along as we listen. Troublemaker[11] and trouble are one. To trouble is to haunt, and a haunting cannot be grasped, only felt. The problem can be grasped, if not resolved. It's strictly nominal, and can be designated. Trouble is free to change form, to embody the problem. The latter can lead to trouble but cannot become it. Trouble has no limit, no end. Like suffering, it is transferable, even and especially upon death. Trouble is what gets you.

The word is an evocation, but it is also a talisman. To summon "trouble" is to replace trouble with the word — to have the word instead of trouble. "Trouble" is a magic word, an incantation that protects the singer, and the listener, from trouble.[12] The word also replaces description. Context in and around the song may bring us closer to the real trouble and its sources, but such investigations also bring us closer to danger and ruin — the danger and ruin of history.[13] "Trouble" is in harm's way, or in the way of harm — it is between the singer and actual trouble. Or the singer keeps us behind him as he faces trouble, turns to whisper "trouble" over his shoulder. If we peek around him we are on our own. Or the singer embodies trouble, stands between us and the real, facing us. "Trouble"[14] is the singer, "Trouble"[15] is the song; trouble[16] is behind the singer, "trouble"[17] is before us. We step around "trouble" to face the real at our own peril. We have been warned by the song.

---

[11] On the title track to his country gospel album *The Troublemaker* (1976), Willie Nelson is the song, which names him, an outlaw hippie Christ, as he sings it.

[12] It might also, as will be explored, protect the singer from the prying I of the listener.

[13] The angel of history's problem is its inability to turn away from the ruin of history, but unlike the angel of history, we have trouble at our backs whether or not we face the ruins.

[14] a name, an embodiment

[15] an eponymous song title, and the substance (insubstantial as it may be) of the song, framed by titular quotation marks

[16] of which he sings

[17] the song, the representation of trouble which we witness

If trouble runs through song it runs through time. The body of Trouble Song, when considered as such, is a single text, the map laid over the territory of history.[18] Time collapses into this text. Trouble Song is its own genre, or it is the collapse of genres. It is genre trouble.[19]

Trouble Songs,[20] like the Trouble Song, is necessarily[21] unfinished.

---

18   Body, text, map — a mixed metaphor, or a signal fluidity.
19   "[T]o make 'gender trouble' is to act up as subtext: that is, to perform *sub*-versions: parody, pastiche, ironic mirrorings, deconstructive replications. … [But to] make real gender trouble is to make genre trouble" (Retallack 112; cf. Butler).
20   Here, let us sing the book, though elsewhere Trouble Songs (no italics) will be treated as a project, ongoing, a song about a song (so the quotation marks have not yet come to roost).
21   and always already

David Lynch, Trouble Man[22]

> *They're well placed for entering into a dream.*
> — David Lynch

A few related moments from *Eraserhead*[23] (1977, that punk year)[24]:

> You're in very bad trouble if you won't cooperate.
> — Mrs. X
> I'm too nervous.
> — Henry Spencer
> They're still not sure it *is* a baby.
> — Mary X

Trouble is contagious.[25] In *Eraserhead,* we see it spread from old-fashioned female-trouble (unanticipated pregnancy) to a mélange (or ménage) of trouble: a family condition. Mrs. X confers the trouble upon Henry as a quasi-Oedipal advance, while

---

22 A visitation from the next world, or the one before that. Lines from films attributed to characters.
23 "A dream of dark and troubling things," as Lynch described it, per Dennis Lim, who covered Lynch's Trouble Songs in *The Man From Another Place* (2015). The above epigraph comes from an unattributed French interview as quoted in Lim (89), in which Lynch describes TV viewers in their living rooms.
24 "The '70s, to me, were about the worst!" Lynch has said, claiming his favorite years to be "the '20s up to 1958, or maybe 1963." He also admits to a fondness for the things in the '80s that recall the '50s (Lim 77). All of which might provide some context for the out-of-time, often dated, and just as frequently repressive quality of gender relations and family romance in his films.
25 Be warned by we who can no longer avoid Trouble Songs, though our aim is to develop more than an awareness of the pink elephant in the room. Let Trouble Songs do what *Trouble Songs* does: dispel trouble while bringing "trouble" to light.

Mary foretells her off offspring, which will not be her burden to bear alone.[26]

Dennis Lim reports, "*Inland Empire* [Lynch's long-form 2006 digital feature] is the story of 'a woman in trouble.'"[27] Lim's analysis of *Blue Velvet* follows a similar tack, delivering:

> Why are there people like Frank? Why is there so much trouble in this world?
> —Jeffrey Beaumont
> So I guess it means there is trouble until the robins come.
> —Sandy Williams

We may ask for trouble, and trouble may reply with a dedicated song: This one's for you, peeker under the sod. What's the hurry?

You have at least the length of this song. And then the robins come.

---

26 On the contrary, she will flip the script and leave Henry with the so-called baby. But not before kneeling down at the foot of the bed, framed behind the bars of the footboard, to rip the floor out from under us. Or is she just pulling her suitcase of troubles from beneath the bed (to *dump 'em in a deep blue sea*)?[a]

    a See Loretta Lynn's "I'm Gonna Pack My Troubles"—from her 1968 album *Here's Loretta Lynn*, previously issued in 1960 as a B-side to "The Darkest Day"—in a 1961 televised performance via YouTube.

27 How does a woman get in trouble, we might ask, though we might better ask how trouble *put its disease in me,* as Dorothy Vallens intones while we head for the troubled waters of *Blue Velvet.*

Trouble Forms: Structure & Approach

We pursue *trouble* through *song* in an extended, exploratory sense of both terms. This includes musicological, ethnographic, historical, linguistic, and critical research relating to the Trouble Songs project. Song-based musicological analysis of folk, blues, gospel, jazz vocal standards, country, and rock[28] grounds and instantiates "trouble" as a culturally evocative term. The trouble lyric is approached as euphemism and cipher, explored in its potential points of reference, which extend from interpersonal and romantic negotiation to race and class struggle. Thus, interrelated chapters concern the nature and persistence of trouble in all its forms and representations.[29] These linked chapters deal with particular songs, poems, novels, critical and cultural theory, sociological investigation, historical documentation and other works, where fields and genres commingle.[30] All cultural and literary forms are discussed under the rubric of Trouble Songs as a way to problematize traditional genre distinctions. For example, blues are considered alongside folk and rock music, allowing these forms to interact rather than isolating works in a particular genre or era. Moreover, no inherent privilege is given to critical or cultural texts, sources, or resources; chronology is not the principle of organization, but a historical perspec-

---

28 to be treated as open song fields — rather than cordoned territories — to be explored, negotiated, extrapolated, conflated

29 Throughout, text and footnotes have a symbiotic, nonhierarchical relationship — a vertical spread. The footnote initiates a below-and-back movement of the eye that corresponds with a movement below the surface of the text, and a movement from the present to a conditional present, and back to what has become the past, moving forward into the present. The footnote is textual time travel, as is the Trouble Songs project (which, like listening to music, is also aural time travel). Trouble Song footnotes coexist and converse with the body of the text, rather than subordinating themselves to the body. They are subtext to the body's context, trouble to the body's songs, chorus to its verse — and vice versa. The footnote is also anchor and suture to the floating text.

30 The song chapters can be read as covers, though they will not be treated as replacements for the songs, which must be heard to be conceived (of).

tive does accumulate across chapters.[31] One of the themes of the Trouble Songs project is that time exists only in retrospect, and is constructed in historical memory. Thus, distinctions among chronological eras are by nature arbitrary, and time collapses into the present, which is continuous and without differentiation. Thinking time is being in time. This arbitrariness of era and genre is signified and nuanced by culture,[32] and is therefore worthy of critical cultural analysis, under the sign of Trouble.[33] Throughout this project, we[34] pursue trouble in order to elaborate its resonance across 20th-century American culture.

> Note: This project has its origin in a short 2005 essay published in *Kitchen Sink* magazine, called "Trouble on the Line" (see Appendix A).

---

[31] With the acknowledgement that we move as history does — ostensibly distinct from but inextricably involved with and affected by what happens.

[32] which (culture) is itself a morphology dependent upon the position(s) of its audience, participants and interlocutors

[33] or the sing of Trouble, or the Song of Trouble, the Trouble Song

[34] This convention (the use of we) is intended to encapsulate the I that formulates this text, along with the reader that co-formulates (and activates) this text, as well as the I that revisits these Trouble Songs. It also relieves "me" from walking around with quotes on "my" shoulders. Here we recall Clarice Lispector's (via her translator, Ronald W. Sousa) *The PASSSION according to G.H.*: "I have always kept one quotation mark to my left and another to my right" (23). Let us put marks around the entire text, and step inside together.

Modes of Trouble — Terms — Elaboration, Embellishment, Embodiment[35]

> *Now heavens. Or should I perhaps give up troubling to correct such nonsense altogether, and simply let my language come out any way it insists upon?*
> — David Markson, *Wittgenstein's Mistress*

Delivery format/conveyance, temporality, part of speech (n. vs. v., etc.), representation/non-representation (and replacement), referential vs. poetic language, vocalization/enunciation: all of these are integral to what is being said (or elided), and to the nature of trouble's appearance (as "trouble," or as inference of trouble).

A semantic constellation: genre, general(ity), generic, gender.[36] Trouble may be a man, a woman, a transgender person, a situation, an atmosphere, a condition — trouble is contingency, in a word. To speak of Trouble Songs is to invite genre trouble (via genre consciousness).[37]

---

35 an extended outline format, a set of expanding propositions, invitations to trouble space
36 A point in the *Oxford English Dictionary*'s constellation of meanings for "gender" binds it to genre: "Kind, sort, class; also, genus as opposed to species. *the general gender*: the common sort (of people)." Compare to "genre":
    a. Kind; sort; style.
    b. *spec.* A particular style or category of works of art; esp. a type of literary work characterized by a particular form, style, or purpose.
37 Once genre enters, the room is gendered (that is, troubled by gender, or gen[d]re).

Trouble[38] may be appropriated, and misappropriated.[39]

Is trouble (inter-)culturally transmittable? Is trouble historically transmittable? Is trouble chrono-logical? That is, can it be dis-

---

38 "We've got to show them we're worse than queer / SUCK MY LEFT ONE SUCK MY LEFT one" (liner notes) hollers Kathleen Hanna on Bikini Kill's "Suck My Left One," from Bikini Kill's self-titled debut EP. At the time (1991), a wave of feminist punk, dubbed riot grrl (later mass-mediated as Riot Grrrl, that third r adding a cartoon growl—or purr), acts up during grunge's USA-via-Seattle, crowd-surfing big splash, as Bikini Kill leads the charge into boy-strewn waters. Defiantly unladylike, Hanna belts out lines like *Eat meat / Hate Blacks / Beat your fucking wife / Its* [sic] *all the same thing* ("Liar"), troubling the waters of American commercial culture and calling women to the stage. The last song on the EP is a live recording of "Thurston Hearts the Who," featuring Molly Neuman (credited as molly germs), who is invited onstage to recite a hostile review while the band plays the song (ostensibly for the first time) behind her. Neuman created the zine *Girl Germs,* along with Allison Wolfe, with whom she formed another influential riot grrl band, Bratmobile. Bikini Kill takes its name from a zine written by Hanna and the band's drummer, Tobi Vail (who will be a founding member of Ladyfest, a feminist nonprofit arts and music festival). At the turn of the millennium, Hanna further troubles genre and gender with Le Tigre (whose albums are bookended by Hanna's Julie Ruin project[a]). The group layers electronic elements, including programmed beats and samples, with minimal traditional rock instrumentation to create feminist agit-pop, accompanied live by multimedia performances. The original trio includes a filmmaker, Sadie Benning, and another zine maker, Johanna Fateman. Benning is replaced by the band's projectionist, JD Samson, between the group's 1999 self-titled debut and its 2001 follow-up, *Feminist Sweepstakes* (both of which are released on the queer label Mr. Lady, itself an invocation of gender trouble). Samson goes on to raise genderqueer awareness in her dance music project (with Johanna Fateman), MEN.

   a The first, self-titled Julie Ruin album precedes Le Tigre's eponymous 1999 debut by a year, anticipating stylistic shifts Hanna will explore with her Le Tigre bandmates. In 2013, nearly a decade after Le Tigre's final studio album, Hanna issues a second Julie Ruin album, *Run Fast,* which is followed in 2016 by *Hit Reset.* Hanna's hiatus (or exile) from music is well documented in Sini Anderson's vital 2013 documentary, *The Punk Singer.*

39 Misappropriation is (an) appropriation.

covered or elaborated along a line of time, according to a logic of transport and association?[40]

Trouble is a hiding place. The singer does not have to reveal what is behind the song. The Trouble Song is a veiled confession: nothing but trouble. Or, it's a veiled threat: nothing but trouble in here. In that sense, is it a threat to the singer, the listener, or both? When is trouble the agent, or the subject, and when is it the object of the song?[41]

If "trouble" replaces trouble, the song might replace the singer (or the subject).[42] The song travels over time, transcending the moment of its conception or documentation, moving out of its context but carrying a[43] context. Judith Butler summarizes the philosophical tradition of mind/body dualism with reference to "relations of political[44] and psychic subordination and hierarchy": "The mind not only subjugates the body, but occasionally entertains the fantasy of fleeing its embodiment altogether" (12). If trouble is the anchor of the flesh, the predicament that is embodiment in an antipathetic world, song—and in particular, Trouble Song—is the entertainment of flight: from trouble, from embodiment, along the float lines of signification.

When "trouble" replaces trouble, the singer enacts a relation to embodiment that the listener uses as a model for her own displacement. She is good and gone in song, as Jason Lytle of Grandaddy sings in "Lost on Yer Merry Way," which begins, *Trouble*

---

40 Yes and no. Discovery leads to (or from) recovery, and an inevitable re-covering; all things cannot be present—or accounted for—at once. This is concept trouble, or the trouble with concept(s).
41 And how does this relate to signification?
42 Cf. Willie Nelson, *The Troublemaker*, which, as noted, (also) (explicitly) replaces the singer with the album. The movie-poster *Is* is silent (and/or replaced by a comma).
43 if not the
44 Here let us say "political" encapsulates—and embodies—the world that is the case, as Wittgenstein has it. Or: The body is the case, and the song will be the body, as "trouble" will be the word that is the case. And: the footnote is the case/song before (and after, and beneath) the case/body.

with a capital T.[45] Escape is a trick of language — in the second verse, the line morphs into *Trouble with people like me,* which is followed by *Tie 'em down and then they vanish instantly.* If the song remains, if it plays over time, the vanishing is a continuous present to the listener.[46]

Why and when does "trouble" appear in songs?[47] How aware of its usage are arrangers[48] and performers of Trouble Songs?

The concern is not just — and not primarily — what "trouble" is (what it means, what it refers to) in a Trouble Song, but to investigate/analyze/diagram/trouble/vet/consider how "trouble" is used grammatically, which pronouns and characters it relates to, who delivers and reports trouble (cf. also subject/object orientation), etc. In his ethnomusicological study of working-class Texans' identification with country music, *Real Country,* Aaron Fox considers modes and representations of affect — what these Texans talk about when they talk about "real country":

> "Feeling" and "relating (to)" are diffuse, integrative, summarizing ideas. These terms, which fulfill a variety of grammatical functions, often appear to refer to essentialized, ineffable properties of social and aesthetic experience: if you have to ask what "feeling" means, in other words, you'll never know, and that's the point. "Feeling" is an inchoate quality of authenticity. But this phenomenological knot can be analytically untangled to reveal an orderly, dynamic, and elegantly binary semantic field. (155)

---

45 *Trouble Songs'* style for quoting lyrics is italics, to indicate they are sung — slanted and inflected — and that they do not belong to the singer (are borrowed, transmitted, paid forward, lost). Quotations from texts other than songs are treated with standard quotation marks.

46 *Ask you just what kind / Of trouble I might find / Tonight out of my... my mind,* Lytle (dis)embodies (and echoes my mind) in "Chartsengrafs."

47 And does it appear as the sign of a disappearance — of trouble, of the singer or subject?

48 We could say writers, and we could say transcribers, or we could invoke conjurers (though perhaps only performers have the power to conjure, even if they need a spell).

Of course, the language of the academic clashes with the phenomenon under consideration, but simply put, Fox is coordinating two fields: verbal expression and embodied emotion. The singer relates to his audience — imparting a lyrical story, articulating emotion, connecting to common experiences — and the audience responds in kind — feeling it, singing along, moving to and being moved by the song.

The trouble singer also presents an "inchoate quality of authenticity" which we — and she — might call "trouble." We can ask what it means, but the singer can't — or won't — tell us any more than her song does. She relates by genre, or generically. Her trouble and ours might not signify the same way, and the Trouble Song accounts for this in its open feel (sic) of meaning. Perhaps *What is trouble?* is not the right question. Instead, the singer asks — or replies — *What's your trouble?*[49] and the audience responds in kind. This rapport is the mutual feeling, the sharing, of trouble.

Retying the knot: What does "trouble" do/mean for the singer vs. the listener(s) — what role does the trouble singer play, and how do listeners charge/change the song (and how is that complicated by the lag and historicity afforded/effected by recording, along with complications of time and race displacement)? Here we (re-)enter the trouble space. Whose trouble is this anyway?

> These are the songs people call "the sad, slow songs," and they typically tell of troubled moments in life: heartbreak, despair, regret, aging, leaving, desire for forgiveness, shame and sin. Such songs evoke an intensely felt sense of location and temporality. (Fox 88)

Consider the ethos and ambience of the Trouble Song as distinguished from a phenomenological classification of songs that

---

49 though it comes out *Trouble, trouble, I've had it all my days*

include "trouble" in their lyrics.[50] Cat Power's *The Covers Record* includes "trouble" songs, but is a holistic collection of Trouble Songs in that the songs are infused with the climate(s) of trouble.[51] It is significant that one of the "trouble" songs (which is also a Trouble Song) is a Dylan cover ("Paths of Victory"), since Dylan is especially attentive to the Trouble Song mode/mood.[52]

---

50 Which is to say, trouble (and gen[d]re) may be in the house — here, consider verse and chorus as stanzas, or rooms — even when "trouble" is not in evidence.
51 troubled also by format for all those listening to *The Covers Record* on CD
52 A list of trouble-saturated musicians and albums would be a long one, but a few notables spring to (this) mind (this moment): *Dusty* (Springfield) *in Memphis,* Judee Sill, Smog, Syd Barrett, Bonnie Prince Billy, Amy Winehouse, Love, Gil Scott-Heron, Ann Peebles — and of course, most of blues and much of country music (a study of the dynamics of trouble in rap and hip hop could overfill its own volume). Every music list is a process of exclusion. The reader of a list makes her own, largely in opposition to the trigger list. All the better. Note also: Trouble might just as likely be a mood as a mode — a passing fancy, or the wake of (if not waking from) one. Dylan has recorded at least 24 songs with some form of "trouble" in the lyrics (and countless Trouble Songs that do not mention the word), several of them far better known than "Paths of Victory," which appears on Dylan's *Bootleg Series, Vols. 1-3 (Rare & Unreleased), 1961-1991.* Dylan has also recorded "Trouble Songs" (songs with "Trouble" in the title) like "Trouble" and "Trouble in Mind," and has avoided "trouble" by replacing it with "worry" in "Someday Blues," his version of Muddy Waters' "Trouble No More" (also worried by the Allman Brothers).

Not Wanting to (Formally)[53] Listen to Trouble Songs[54]

Do Trouble Songs resist analysis? I would rather talk about trouble (and "trouble") and Trouble Songs than analyze a Trouble Song. Is this like explaining a magic trick?[55] Worse: explaining magic? Yes and no. This is the ambivalence of the music writer.[56] The song gives itself to the listener: Even in its reticence, it gives its reticence.[57] Here is the extant link between poetry and song. Analysis is betrayal in a way that conversation, especially sacramental conversation, is not. Academic prose is an abomination, except in that it unabashedly disregards the constraints of genre — it rejects the pre-eminent eloquence of linguistic art while disavowing its own art (except in moments of excess, e.g., Harold Bloom's poem at the end of *The Anxiety of Influence,* which if not a work of art, is the pretense of a work of art).[58] Besides, it is better (or just as good) to remember a Trouble Song than it is

---

53 as a matter of research practice — taking notes (hip static[a]) vs. listening
    a as Allen Ginsberg referred to audience feedback during poetry readings
54 in which you and I appear together, as a veil is lifted
55 In conversation, Ira Livingston relays a parable of (and for) postmodernism, a string from which to hang: We can show how a magic trick works without ruining the magic (or the trick). And we can tell the future without spoiling the plot. If all this foot dragging drags you down, translocate to Part Two, where we get over it.
56 The music writer we call to task wants to distinguish herself from "music journalists ... who move ever more quickly toward the domestication of radical sound" (Moten, *In the Break,* 224). But we call attention as well to what Moten describes as "that resistance of the object — to dis/appearance or interpretation — that constitutes the essence of performance" (225). Trouble Songs typically arrive as records of a performance, which we stage as a re-appearance of song, singer, audience, and "trouble."
57 And "it is this resistance that demands analysis" (Moten 226).
58 Less defensive gestures might also trouble the line between academic criticism and art. Rachel Zolf has commented (in conversation) on the linguistic beauty of theory. Is the work of Deleuze and Guattari, Butler, Derrida, Barthes, Jameson, Kristeva, and/or your favorite theorists a product of or assimilable in the academy, and what is the academy, and what is art, and criticism, etc., &/but here we are mooning over theory in an investigation of song which owes its blood flow, should there be any, to poetics (and linguistics, &c.). RIP and long live theory.

to listen to one, and it is better by far to listen than it is to speak. And if one must speak (and this ought to be one's only appearance here), s/he ought to listen first.

History

> Classic blues attempts a universality that earlier blues forms could not even envision. But with the attainment of such broad human meaning, the meanings which existed in blues only for Negroes grew less pointed. (Jones 87)

In *Blues People*, LeRoi Jones (not yet Amiri Baraka) attends the transition between the individuated, private "primitive blues" that followed emancipation and the subsequent white supremacist reaction that was Jim Crow — the transition between integral developments in blues as a result of privacy and independence, to the extent that they were newly available to Black Americans in the late 19th century, and the nuanced disillusionment of qualified freedom — and the professionalization of blues music that followed. As Black Americans were both relatively free to move around the country and desperately (and itinerantly) in search of work, blues became an occupation (or a side job), rather than primarily or only a mode of personal expression made possible by the solitary alienation of the free(d) Black American.[59]

---

[59] It should be noted here that Jones distinguishes between "classic" and "country" blues singers: "While the country singers accompanied themselves usually on guitar or banjo, the classic blues singers usually had a band backing them up" (90). He also notes that classic blues, which was dominated by great female singers like Bessie Smith and Ma Rainey, was recorded years before country blues singers, who were "almost always men" (91), made records. Jones notes that the "best-known country singers were wanderers" seeking employment, while women could not and did not need to move around the way men did. Not only were there societal and familial restrictions on her movement, but a woman could "almost always obtain domestic employment," which meant she did not need to travel for work (91). Of course, there was a sense of glamour and prestige associated with the entertainment field and traveling shows, which was a draw for classic blues singers, "providing an independence and importance not available in other areas open to them — the church, domestic work, or prostitution" (93). In any case, as Angela Davis points out in her critical study on Rainey, Smith and Billie Holiday, *Blues Legacies and Black Feminism* (1998), "Most women ... were denied the option of taking to the road" (19). Davis also

If emancipation allowed Black Americans to be by themselves, together or separately,[60] and to cultivate private lives not strictly circumscribed by servitude, it also led to the development of a public blues form that communicated in a way that was not at issue in private blues. Black American slaves were not allowed to freely express their interiority in all its complexity, but their experiences were also limited by their circumstances. They did not have free time; generations of slaves born in America only knew servitude, and had little more to sing about.[61] Emancipated Black Americans had broadened if not necessarily liberated — from racism, hunger, destitution — experiences. As blues developed from personal and personalized self-gratifying expression to public performance, its modes of signification also developed and diversified. The audience inflects the material, or the performer inflects the material toward (and away from) the audience. Perhaps before there is an audience, and particularly

> elaborates on the rights and prerogatives that were and were not available to Black blues musicians after emancipation. Political and economic freedom were not available, so these musicians exercised (and sang about) the freedom they did have: the (gender qualified) ability to travel, and sexual agency (which Davis's subjects asserted as a freedom they shared with male counterparts) denied them under the conditions of slavery. Davis goes on to connect themes of travel in the music of Black female blues musicians with sexual autonomy, and discusses the ways in which these songs "permitted the women's blues community — performers and audiences alike — to engage aesthetically with ideas and experiences that were not accessible to them in real life" (66). As Davis explains, this promotes the development of Black cultural consciousness and the pursuit of proto-feminist liberation, as "dominant gender politics within black consciousness are troubled and destabilized" (67). Here is an emergent early 20th-century strategy of gender trouble situated within shifting genre parameters: gender trouble becoming genre trouble.

60 though perhaps no one can be denied the privacy of her mind, or of sleep — not for long

61 Nor were they allowed to sing of much else — so that, for example, a song about sexual or liberatory desire must be sublimated and encoded within the work song, and delivery to the hereafter might stand in for escape from the land of servitude. In *The Grey Album: On the Blackness of Blackness* (2012), Kevin Young writes about Frederick Douglas's analysis of slave-era spirituals, "[T]hese songs were not just about Canaan or the afterlife, but about Canada and the life after slavery."

an audience composed of Others, *there is no* material — or, in Jones's terms, there is expression, but no artifact (30), no song as song object.[62]

At any rate, by the early 20th century, blues becomes public exhibition, and it takes on a universal inflection that is "less obscure to white America," a "classic blues" that is "less involuted, and certainly less *precise*" (Jones 87). Considered in the "trouble" light,[63] this universality is analogous to a generality of reference that charges lyrical utterance. *What trouble? Your trouble.* The singer can protect herself while forming a performative bond with the listener. In effect, she sings to herself[64] *while* singing to others, but the song does not necessarily sound or mean the same thing to both parties. Still, the self- and other-audience both inflect the song. As Gertrude Stein has it in *Everybody's Autobiography,* she writes for herself and strangers. This emergent form of disjunction with and from the self[65] is what leads Luc Sante, in "The Invention of the Blues," to describe the blues[66] as an important development in American modernism. Here we are spanning time, but it is a contingent, cumulative, even self-reflexive time. Blues forms are certainly aware that they are being followed (by themselves and by other, stranger selves).

---

62 This is complicated by the race record era of the 1920s, during which time country blues singers were eventually recorded (again, after classic blues was recorded). Not only did the proliferation of phonographic records provide a blues artifact, but it circulated country blues, making its more private expressive sensibilities public. "Classic blues was entertainment and country blues, folklore" (Jones 105), but both had become artifactual (and commodified) by the late '20s. They also became ripe fields for floating signification, doublespeak and encryption, all under the sign of accessibility.
63 which projects and reveals trouble
64 as the song sings to her, or sings her
65 which flows along the line of alienation specific to commodity forms in production and consumption, to which performance points
66 and more specifically, country blues, particularly because he concerns himself with the innovations of individual, primarily male, itinerant musicians

Trouble Song as Speech Act & Magic Language

The Trouble Condition & The Talismanic Effect

> *But when a man suspects any wrong, it sometimes happens that if he be already involved in the matter, he insensibly strives to cover up his suspicions even from himself. And much this way it was with me. I said nothing, and tried to think nothing.*
> — Herman Melville, *Moby Dick*

> *These signs of distress signify distress only indirectly: what they indicate first is the effort to avoid showing distress.*
> — Chris Fujiwara, *The World and Its Double: The Life and Work of Otto Preminger*

> *The artist's sitters present themselves with an attitude and a sartorial flair, that, as the critic Kobena Mercer has argued, attract the gaze yet also defend against primitivist projection, carving out a space where the self and its aesthetic construction can take center stage.*
> — Huey Copeland, "Barkley L. Hendricks: Figures and Grounds"

> *[I]n ... West African cultural traditions ... naming things, forces and modes ... is a means of establishing magical (or, in the case of the blues, aesthetic) control over the object of the naming process.*
> — Angela Y. Davis, *Blues Legacies and Black Feminism*

Just as a man (and a character in a film) might hide his distress in a gesture of distress, a singer might hide[67] his troubles — and himself — in an aestheticized (and potentially anesthetizing) evocation of "trouble."

"Historical images, like mass-cultural ones, are hardly innocent of associations: indeed, it is because they are so laden that they are used" (Hal Foster, "Against Pluralism" 29). So too is "trouble" laden and useful. But does it necessarily reference iden-

---

67   or cover

tification in the listener? And if "trouble" operates as a shield for or against trouble, might it also operate as a shield against the listener (or for trouble in another sense), a way to protect the private concerns of the singer or speaker — a way to protect trouble?[68] Indeed (and in addition), "trouble" might protect the speaker from the singer, whether or not by design of the songwriter.

Consider the case of the cover, in which the singer might not (be able to) access the original trouble, or might more or less intentionally redirect "trouble" to her own trouble (or her own indication of trouble, which may itself be enmeshed in character representation). In this cluster-case, representation merges with production (and/or reproduction). What of Walter Benjamin's aura remains in such handed-down "trouble," and how might this be further complicated by cultural appropriations of Trouble Songs (by singers and by listeners)? If the aura or authenticity of "trouble" fades in this exchange, does the Trouble Song paradoxically become a more powerful (or, at least, effective) shield or talisman against trouble? Furthermore and at any rate, in all of these possibilities and contingencies, the Trouble Song may absorb the condition *as trouble* (that is, as part of its trouble condition).

The poet John Ashbery sings of this trouble condition in his long poem "Self-Portrait in a Convex Mirror":

As Parmigianino did it, the right hand
Bigger than the head, thrust at the viewer
And swerving easily away, as though to protect
What it advertises. ... (68)

In the trouble light, we are tempted to ascribe the Parmigianino convexity effect[69] to a distortive affect of trouble. As with any cover, Ashbery converts his subject with an objectifying gaze,

---

68 A related concern revealed (or, paradoxically, uncovered) by this conceit: Is "trouble" the shield, or is the singer the shield, or is the song the shield?
69 abetted — or conjured — by Ashbery

which is the troubling of representation, if not the trouble of representation.

In the next book Ashbery published after *Self-Portrait in a Convex Mirror*, 1977's *Houseboat Days*, the second poem, "The Other Tradition," calls trouble by name as it concludes

> ... You found this
> Charming, but turned your face fully toward night,
> Speaking into it like a megaphone, not hearing
> Or caring, although these still live and are generous
> And all ways contained, allowed to come and go
> Indefinitely in and out of the stockade
> They have so much trouble remembering, when your
>   forgetting[70]
> Rescues them at last, as a star absorbs the night. (3)

We might look back in search of the referent of "this,"[71] and we can attribute it to a forest, or the idea of a forest, or the way "the idea of a forest had clamped itself / Over the minutiae of the scene," and we will certainly find other candidates for "this"-ness, and perhaps this is also part of the trouble condition. We too (like they[72], whoever they[73] are) have trouble remembering, or we hone in on "this" "remembering," losing ourselves.

---

70 Some poets indicate when a stanza break does or does not coincide with a page break, but few indicate whether a hanging line is a matter of typography or intention. See Lyn Hejinian's *The Cell* for examples of clearly intentional hanging lines. Compare to the poems in C.K. Williams's *Tar*, which habitually hang, perhaps only (if not certainly) by exceeding the width of the page.

71 Here we are tempted to throw clarity to the wind and say "'this' referent,' which improves upon the range and flow of sense.

72 See Joshua Clover's chapbook (with accompanying multivocal music-mashup CD), *Their Ambiguity* (2003).

73 "Their Ambiguity" also appears in the collection *the totality for kids*. Warning: Their ambiguity will remain, though they might refer to poetry and revolution. Note also: "The content of the town is our pleasure; everything that remains is form, // though one could say the same thing about the totality for kids" (55).

So there is pleasure in "trouble," just as trouble itself may be a source of pleasure, at least temporarily.

Genre Trouble

Blues is a music with trouble on its mind. The concerns and preoccupations of blues address — sing from, sing to — emotional and material conditions that may inform the Trouble Song. The question of who can sing the blues — which people, which culture has a right to the form, or even the mode — gets us into genre trouble,[74] which is where we want to be if we are to locate the Trouble Song transmission in the present. Jones kills two blues with one stone when he writes of "the peculiar social, cultural, economic, and emotional experience of a black man in [1920s] America." He continues:

> The idea of a white blues singer seems an even more violent contradiction of terms than the idea of a middle-class blues singer. The materials of blues were not available to the white American, even though some strange circumstance[75] might prompt him to look for them. It was as if these materials were secret and obscure, and blues a kind of ethno-historic rite as basic as blood. (148)

On one hand, this makes us wonder how to categorize the country blues (and the "Country Blues") of (white) 1920s Virginia mountain balladeer[76] Dock Boggs. On another hand, we wonder about later blues-inflected singers like Karen Dalton and Chan Marshall, who might be double-struck in Jones's formulation ("black man").

As Luc Sante will later do in "The Invention of the Blues,"[77] Jones talks about the blues, in its classic form, having a "twelve-bar, three-line, AAB structure"[78] (Jones 62; cf. Sante 177). Sante

---

74 and/or casts genre in the light of cultural critique, if not ethnology
75 trouble, indeed
76 as Greil Marcus characterizes him in *Invisible Republic* (20)
77 As it is published in his 2007 collection *Kill All Your Darlings*, the essay carries the compositional date range of 1994–2002.
78 AAB refers to an end-rhyme scheme and verse structure as well as describing the whole-line, perfect-rhyme (repetition)-plus-punchline blues form.

goes on to say, "Although the term 'blues' came to be applied to any minor-key lament—in the 1920s and '30s to almost any kind of song—the authentic blues songs are those that hew to this structure" (177, 178).[79] No music is authentic for long, and authenticity is a historically acquired quality. And yet, music is made. Songs follow other songs, stealing from one another, appropriating and misappropriating terms (and lines) and forms. Surprise in song is a function of recognition: It is the strange or wayward element, this mismatched detail, the anachronism or stray, the wrongness that fits in a way that changes the blood (flow)[80] of the listener.[81] The recognizable is made strange, but the strange is also revealed to be recognizable, or rendered as such. As the strange is recognized, it is incorporated into experience. As the song travels, as it is re-encountered, the surprise is transformed into nuance, into style. This is what Sante calls innovation, which is based on deliberate decisions of individual artists, as distinguishable from "the inherited or instinctive moves of people following tradition without questioning or altering it" (196). However, here we also refer to the movement of the song as it finds us here, today. We recognize the way the song has come, to the extent that we know its (and our) history. It is

---

A classic example is "Downhearted Blues," written by Lovie Austin and Alberto Hunter, and performed by Bessie Smith:
    Trouble, trouble, I've had it all my days (A)
    Trouble, trouble, I've had it all my days (A)
    It seems like trouble going to follow me to my grave (B)
In this case, the *AAB* structure can be described as AAA, in terms of end rhyme (if the days/grave slant-rhyme is recognized). We might imagine an original (here: debut) performance in which the singer calls the A-line, the audience repeats it with her, and the singer answers with the B-line. In that case, we might imagine a floating-lyric composition, where the audience recognizes some or all of the parts—taken from "the great body of ambient tropes known collectively as the folk-lyric" (Sante 185)—but the whole is original.

79 Sante also identifies the structure with "line length of five stressed syllables" (177).
80 as singing changes the flow of blood, bulging the veins of the neck, pouring oxygenated blood on the brain, and as listening affects the heart's behavior
81 and again, the singer is also a listener, the listener a singer

an artifact covered with fingerprints which texture its surface, and contribute to the depth of its surface. The song sings to what we know, but it also sings the past away, in its insistence that it has come for us, that it came for us all along. That it encodes a past that acts on us is as important in the moment we encounter the song as our apprehension of any turn of phrase or musical gesture. As we sing along, as we carry the song to others, we aid its travel, and we add (our baggage) to its cargo, further burdening it with the marks of our touch.

Blues, whether classic or derivative, sing trouble. In blues, we find Trouble Songs. We also find them in country, in rock, in folk and rap and anywhere else we find songs, and language, and "trouble." We also find trouble where we cannot locate "trouble." The Trouble Song is an example, or a mode, more than a genre — just as a particular blues is also a song, one that is perceived within a necessarily limiting generic category, and may be heard outside those bounds.[82] We hear a song as blues until it gets hold of us, and then we don't care what it's called. We can only sing. If genre is a claim to contested terrain, the Trouble Song rolls through that terrain, gathering, mulching and fertilizing its grounds. The process does not tend toward purity, but rather admixture and cross-pollination. Borders are traversed, and territories are ultimately reconfigured. Maps, like songs, change.

---

[82] We can also, if only for a moment, hear songs or parts of songs *into* the blues, even if they float on outside of it. And, of course, we might hear (or sing) the blues as a poem.

I'm New Here: The Trouble With Covers

If contemporary covers[83] risk attrition, or the loss of potency, there are still examples of amplification, of powering up. Johnny Cash did it with Nine Inch Nails' "Hurt,"[84] dialing bathos to pathos. Every singer wants to make it her own, just as every listener makes it her own — again, the listener commands and informs the singer, a ritual enacted at the end of every rock show, when the hits are called out by the audience.[85] Post-Cash, Gil Scott-Heron amplified an already affective version, making Smog's "I'm New Here" sing truer.[86] Homage and interpretation, Scott-Heron's cover reveals the aspiration of Bill Callahan's (convincing) pretensions. Also distinguishing itself from the "Hurt"/"Hurt" dialectic, Scott-Heron's version of "I'm New Here" leaves open the option/desire of hearing the "original" again, even while casting quotes around it.[87] Which is to say

---

83 Surely the cover is a 20th-century notion of an old practice, and the genius of that practice is latent in the contemporary cover. In the folk lyric (or floating lyric) tradition described by Greil Marcus and Luc Sante, two songs with the same title may carry divergent or wholly different lyrics, just as distinct songs with different titles may share (and recirculate, and recontextualize) recognizable phrases. As long as there have been singers with audiences of any size, there have likely been songs that served as calling cards. From our 21st-century perspective, songs have specific origins and writers, and to sing another person's song is to cover it (or steal it). We'd like to suggest that songs are made of wind and breath, and just as lyrics still float in that wind, the wind passes through the singer's breath.

84 on Cash's *American IV: The Man Comes Around* (2002), part of a six-session covers clinic on song stealing; the song originally appeared at the end of Nine Inch Nails' *The Downward Spiral* (1994)

85 The singer deflects the call by substituting a cover for the hit.

86 Originally, the song appeared on Smog's final album, 2005's *A River Ain't Too Much to Love* (subsequently, Bill Callahan recorded under his name); Scott-Heron made it the title track of his "comeback" album from 2010 (he had not made a studio album in 15 years, and his previous album followed a 12-year hiatus). *No matter how far wrong you've gone / You can always turnaround /.../ And you may come full circle and be new here again,* Scott-Heron sang with an authority Callahan cannot muster, despite how his (Callahan's) version sounds.

87 Bill Callahan's cover of the Smog version, "performed at the benefit Letters to Santa, Second City, Chicago, December 15, 2010," according to the You-

there is a difference between making it your own and stealing it, as there are different modes of stealing it. Both Cash and Scott-Heron steal it, but in the latter case, the stolen object is, magically, still in its original position, if not its original state.

Tube video posted December 19, 2010, turns around on itself, a reflection of and on a reflection, an eye reflecting itself in a clogged sing (*sic*). The song is no longer his, but he remembers it well. It's still in his set (better for the wear) as of a June 26, 2016 performance early in a three-day, six-show run at Baby's All Right in Brooklyn, NY, where he appears to be covering Scott-Heron covering Smog, in tribute to Scott-Heron.

The Incantation of Trouble

The Silver Jews' "Trains Across the Sea" (1994) begins with a summons that is also a dismissal: *Troubles, no troubles, on the line*. It's a magic trick, a sleight of line, in which troubles appear only to be shuffled away as the song proceeds, a train of thought disappearing over an ocean of time. In an earlier act of telephonic now you see it, now you see, Gil Scott-Heron's "Lady Day and John Coltrane" (1971) stages a failure to conjure away the singer/listener's troubles. If "you ... call on" the music of Billie Holiday and Coltrane, *They'll wash your troubles, your troubles, your troubles away*. If the first "troubles" summons troubles (and implicates the soiled listener) in order to dismiss them (and make the listener (come) clean), and the second "troubles" is less a negation than a reiteration of what has been washed away, the third "troubles" sounds desperate to make it so. The song ends with a deluge of "your troubles,"[88] and by then we have been washed away with the singer and the troubles he's shared.

That's where the "troubles" are. Trouble itself resides in the next song,[89] "Home Is Where the Hatred Is." Here, there's no "trouble" to guard him/us. The word would be a home, and *it might not be such a bad idea if I never ... went home again*. Not even Lady Day or John Coltrane can wash these troubles away, and the singer can't bring himself to say the word anymore, knowing the spell won't work. Here trouble is a habit, and trouble is the source of the habit.[90] It's accumulation as attrition, returns diminishing to the point of no return.

---

88 Scott-Heron repeats "your troubles" 11 times, including the reiteration of the entire line — *They'll wash your troubles away* — to close out the song.
89 on the album *Pieces of a Man*
90 *Home is where the needle marks / Try to heal my broken heart*

Trouble Is a Lonesome Town, Lee Hazlewood

Trouble can keep you from home, and trouble can be home. A country concept album — or a concept country album — about a town called Trouble, this 1963 debut LP links its songs with Hazlewood's resonant narration. The album is an evocation,[91] summoning the atmosphere of Anywheresville through the ether of western Americana. The cover art is a rust-orange map overlaid with the script, "You won't find it on any map, but take a step in any direction and you'r [sic] in trouble." Next to that is a snapshot of Hazlewood sitting on train tracks that recede into the distance.[92] He casually embraces a guitar case as he prepares to light a cigarette. He is clean-cut, if more Bogart-faced than fresh faced, and has not yet cultivated his trademark shaggy hair and mustache as the Sonny Bono of country (in looks, if not — quite — aesthetics). The album is an amiable radio show of country tropes and cowboy humor, a cartoon drama of good and bad (if not good and evil). The spoken interludes are so low-toned and deep-voiced as to be pointillist, providing the listener with a warm buzz that carries over into the po-faced but bouncy tunes. It's easy to imagine profane, late-night, non-LP versions of just about every song, to the extent that the album sounds like a sanitized version of what the singer withholds.

The album ends with Hazlewood singing *trouble* with heavy reverb emerging from the harmonica that operates throughout the album as the call of the train. We are now leaving Trouble…[93]

---

91 or a charter, a claim to stylistic territory or format (which Hazlewood would revisit and rework as a heartbreak sequence eight years later on *Requiem for an Almost Lady,* which also featured narrative interludes)

92 We expect Johnny Cash's *Orange Blossom Special* (1965) cover to appear in that distance, catching a light. (In any case, it's another cover for Cash.)

93 perhaps headed for "A Stop at Willoughby," somewhere off on the horizon, a place where we can jump off, the last station in The Twilight Zone

History, Continued

A cover song represents — and re-presents — history. In deed, "trouble" is a cover for trouble. How does the "original" song represent history? It changes as we move away from — and back toward — it.[94] It, which is history. We, who make (up) history.

The context of history travels with our perspective on history.[95] It rides the same train of thought. But there are other trains, other passengers, other compartments:

> This "return to history" is ahistorical for three reasons: the context of history is disregarded, its continuum is disavowed, and conflictual forms of art and modes of production are falsely resolved in pastiche. Neither the specificity of the past nor the necessity of the present is heeded. Such a disregard makes the return to history also seem to be a liberation *from* history. And today [ca. 1985] many artists do feel that, free of history, they are able to use it as they wish. Yet, almost self-evidently, an art form is specific: its meaning is part and parcel of its period and cannot be transposed innocently. (Foster, "Against Pluralism" 16)

But we are never innocent in and around Trouble Songs. Whether we hear or sing them,[96] and despite what they withhold, or promise to withhold, Trouble Songs dispel any illusion of innocence.[97] The reassuring smile in profile conceals the knowing grin in shadow.

---

[94] Angels of history, we face away from the future but back toward it, so we cannot see the future until it is past; we take the edge of history — the future — with us as we run back to the ruins.

[95] a synchronic view from a diachronic train — where we sit in any car on a long, long trip

[96] and we are always singing, always listening

[97] We all know trouble, even if we didn't know trouble when it walked in.

"Trouble" vs. "Remember"

Without an object, there is a generic metonymy, which is to say, without a referent, the sign becomes (replaces) the object. "Remember," sings David Bowie, in a song ("Blue Jean") in which speaking and singing are conflated, as are remembering and memory, so that what he is saying is what he says. This is history as trouble, or "history" as "trouble." Thus "Remember" is left to hang,[98] but is self-contained, a generic sensuality, self-reflection. It is the word that speaks itself and goes nowhere.

---

[98] or perhaps refer back to the line "I just met a girl named Blue Jean," so the song's pointing is a pose that indicates itself, just-only and just-now. Or perhaps (also) "Remember" refers not to the spoken throwaway "they always let you down when you need 'em" that follows after the chasmal pause, but the preceding revelation that "she got a camouflaged face and no money." What is there, then, to remember but the coin of the refrain, if it is locatable (/in the pocket)?

I MUST BE THE DEVIL'S DAUGHTER

"Troubled Waters," Cat Power

They surround "Kingsport Town" on one side. Unrecognizable on the other side is the Stones' "(I Can't Get No) Satisfaction," which has no chorus to call it by. The roughness LeRoi Jones ascribes to untutored blues is there in Chan Marshall's delivery, and she knows it, just like Karen Dalton knew it. They are interlopers and appropriators or genuine sufferers or just good singers, another kind of authenticity to pack with listening hard at the songs. *Do you remember me / I remember you quite well,* Marshall concludes in "Kingsport Town," shouting across registers to complete David Bowie's "Blue Jean" thought,[99] before announcing herself as "the devil's daughter" while she bridges the gap into "Troubled Waters." She sounds farther off than the previous song, because she must be, as she tells us. She has descended below the surface of the song. She has sunk below the cover. She will drown, nearly as an aside, in that "troubled water." We barely hear her whenever she confronts the troubled water in which she'll subside. She tells us again, in case we missed it, because we missed it. That's all she says, because the song is over. Only after she has drowned does she emerge "Naked if I Want To." After her "Sweedeedee," she will disappear in her own "In This Hole," and that's all for side one, but it's not all the trouble on *The Covers Record*.[100]

---

[99] That is, to answer his song.
[100] "Troubled Waters" is song three on side one. On side two's third song, "Red Apples," she goes down to the river in the first line, re-enacting her descent to the devil's (troubled) waters on the other side. As in a chorus, she repeats herself. She goes down to meet the widow, and she is the devil's daughter.

"Paths of Victory," Cat Power

She comes at it from opposite[101] sides of the keyboard. Her hands skip toward and away from each other. "Trails… troubles" doesn't catch it. There are at least two hitches in her "troubles" (that is, two if you don't consider the inaugural hitch). Before you know it, troubles are over.[102]

---

101 (or distant, or separate)
102 Bob who?

Discomfort & the Cover Condition

Where do "I" stand[103] in relation to trouble and Trouble Songs? Am I the prying I from which the singer protects herself, or am I the I to whom the singer offers protection from or commiseration for trouble?

The speaker in a Trouble Song, or in Trouble Songs,[104] performs a related discomfort. S/he is out of place, caught (/done) wrong. S/he doesn't belong there. Neither do we.[105]

This relates to the trouble of the speaker in a Trouble Song, but perhaps primarily as fantasy. The singer may be unsure whether to reveal (or unleash) trouble, but as singer, s/he cannot help it. The listener does not know if the song is for him, but he grasps it, or has the song in his power, or is under the spell of the song, whether it acknowledges him or not. Can he justify his apprehension? The recording is always a simulacrum of communion.[106] The singer is and is not there, and to the extent that the singer is there, the listener may be there, but there is somewhere else. This is part of the cover condition, in which the appropriator of trouble discourse must question her stake in trouble, and must also invest herself in or charge trouble to bring off the Trouble Song (or risk being an inadvertent charm against trouble, by getting nowhere near it, or by calling faintly to it).[107]

---

103 and where does "I" stand

104 again, we hover in generica, genre space, part of a contingency

105 As in our preliminary visits to the graveyard, where we might as well already be ghosts, we haunt the Trouble Song as much as we sing or listen to it.

106 Or: The singer and song are real, but the recording is a simulation — it fakes it(self).

107 There is no apparent risk of conjuration as Edie Brickell sings of troubled — that is, shallow — water in "What I Am" (1988); and as Natalie Merchant of 10000 Maniacs calls *trouble me* ("Trouble Me," 1989), seeking an edge (*disturb me with all your cares*); and as Cat Stevens is set free of "Trouble" (1970) when he renounces music (and, presumably, "Trouble," along with "Cat Stevens") ca. 1977, though he (as Yusuf Islam) has troubled that disavowal with his gradual return to music beginning in the 1990s. Later, Kristin Hersh will recast the spell in her 2001 cover.

"Good Intentions Paving Company," Joanna Newsom

How I said to you honey just open your heart
When I've got trouble even opening a honey jar
And that right there is where we are

Honey here is jelly roll, blues porn, a promise and an admission. In classic blues, *I make the best jelly roll in town* is brag and come on; in another era, *I can't open my own honey jar* is as much admission[108] as provocation.[109] This is *sorry* as well as *you're never gonna get it (again)*. You had it — you were it — and now I'm singing away from here (read: you). Still, the song lingers, the story draw(l)s out. It's love after the fact — making love out of what's gone.[110] To say *I wanted you to pull over and hold me 'til I can't remember my own name* is to say *you didn't*. Here we are where we ended up: The Good Intentions Paving Company,[111] companied by compensatory horns that lead us out.

The road is paved with lost advances — or/and advancements. Relationships are big (or little) business *and that right there is where we are*. This coupon is good for one free verse. This song is in stead of one (more) good time. Something happened but what is it? You left but you left your self (or (your) trouble) here. Every good motto leaves itself at the door. Don't slam the car on your way out. The song is cloying in that it has no trouble opening a honey jar. Listen: it's still going on.

---

108 and sign of the times
109 *Hello my old country hello* is as well a taunt and flirt at the old man
110 verbing and reverbing across a verse treated like a chorus — *Won't you love me a spell*, which is to say the saying makes a happening, though *no amount of talking is gonna soften the fall*. Language, as real as it is, is not reality.
111 As Bellow writes to Roth with reference to TGIPC, circa 1984, "[I] fucked up again."

Trouble in Dreams, Destroyer

Okay... Susan... Oh... True[112]

Your head gets filled with that stuff. "Trouble" is right there on the cover, but where is it in the songs? Everywhere and nowhere. *Seriously, terror advances.* Dreams can't be grasped either. You reach for it with "Foam Hands": *I didn't know what time it was at all.* That's the fourth song, and the third began when *The State cut off my arms,* so these Foam Hands may be prosthetic. No wonder we can't feel anything. You, I, we... are in trouble. *True love regrets to inform you there are certain things you must do to perceive his face in the stains on the wall.* Part of the trouble seems to be the song sings to us like a dream. We've given up seeking Destroyer's Dan Bejar[113] behind whatever mask he's wearing, so it might as well be love taunting us with vagary, wagging its Foam Hands at the cum stains on the wall.

You... Caution

Beware the company you reside in many times,[114] a mantra someone's clearly not listening to. *Though, in some small way, we're all traitors to our own kind.* This is certainly the trouble condition, or as George Orwell sang it, *Under the spreading chestnut tree, I sold you and you sold me.* Or, Destroyer again, *Who amongst us has left these things undone? Who let these animals into my kingdom?* Indeed, we are drenched in trouble. We're wet with something... but not tears, we're too far gone for tears. *The problem*[115] *as I see it, I was messed up on a tangent that was wrong. They mix*

---

112 these being the first words of each of side one's songs
113 like Smog's Callahan (and Cat Power's Chan Marshall, and The Mountain Goats' John Darnielle), Bejar essentially uses his band name in place of his own; in the tradition of solo artists, he may or may not play with others, but it's his vision, his concept and his persona that move through the songs on a Destroyer album
114 according to the lyric sheet, seven times (spelled out) plus one *Beware...*
115 "Trouble" won't show, but here's his troublesome cousin, drunk on excuses.

'em strong and I was partial to the feeling. Where were we? In the kitchen, making out with someone we'd rather not see. "Shooting Rockets" is borrowed from Swan Lake's repertoire, Bejar's side project supplying his main vehicle for a change.[116]

Common... See... The

A comet of scars or *A commoner's scars*, as the lyric sheet corrects us: either way we're in trouble. *[A] degenerate drunk on war graves, saying—"Guide me, misty poet!"* We all know poets can only lead us astray.[117] *O brave monster! Lead the way*, as we've heard it all before. Part of the trouble is all the drinking. Now we know what wets us, or keeps us from being dry. *See the rain falling down from the sky to its death, smashed on the street in despair, somewhere over there I swear!* Well, maybe it *is* just rain, says the weeping (drunk) man. But this talk of despair and death, and this ingenuine attention grabbing—it's trouble, I tell you. *You always had a problem flowing down rivers* is the cousin again[118] filling in, making excuses. Water everywhere, and nothing left to drink. *[S]o we went down to the store* in "Leopard of Honor" (having left dry "Rivers" behind), when what do we have here? *Remove that wretched writing from the wall.* Perhaps the stains our Foam Hands rubbed weren't seminal at all. *I didn't know why. I guess I was high.* So's that the trouble? Or, no "trouble," and no language either. The song breaks down to *bah dum bah dah* vocalese that will reappear on the next EP, and the LP after that...[119] Meanwhile, the side is over.

---

116 As a "secret" member of the indie-pop supergroup The New Pornographers, Bejar has supplied not only some of the more inspired numbers on each album, but he has contributed songs (or song sketches) from the diagrammatic first Destroyer album, *City of Daughters*.

117 *Poets always lie to you*, or *I'm tired of poets' lies*, or *Don't listen to poets*, or *Don't let poets lie to you*, Björk says, clutching a TV in an interview we can no longer locate.

118 and Cousin Again

119 "Bay of Pigs," from *Bay of Pigs*, and "Bay of Pigs (*detail*)," from *Kaputt*, respectively

I… Libby's

I was high as a kite! I was never coming home! I was… well, you know how it goes. *What devilry the source of this screaming?* This is, of course, a curse, a whole chorus of them. *And I couldn't believe how loud it was.* And here come more non-linguistic vocalizations. The language leaves us as the album spins to a close. If "trouble" represents (and replaces) trouble, "bah dah dum" removes the burden from language. Even the voice is music. But what happens when the vocalese carries the weight of articulation that's bowed the back of every song on the album? Where has this linguistic pressure come from — as he sings *You've been wasted from the day of wandering and boozing and sleeping outside … You've been fucking around* — ? It comes from our dreams of ourselves, and from our selves torn from dreams every day. That's the trouble.[120] *The light holds a terrible*[121] *secret. Oh, the light!*

---

[120] just as the tension and disjunction between intention and action is the trouble; just as language vs. meaning is the trouble
[121] another one of trouble's troublemaking cousins, posing its own problem, less resolvable than "problem," because less substantial, a mere quality, but, turning back on itself, a terrible one

Part Two

I KNOW A PLACE WHERE THERE'S STILL SOMETHING GOING ON

"Trouble" Songs

Trouble may appear in a title and disappear in a song. "Trouble" may sneak up in a song without warning. Trouble may escape a song in a later version. Trouble may be audible in a song without "trouble." Might trouble also elude a "Trouble" Song?

We've (foot)noted (cover) versions in which trouble is only a word, but considering our allowance of Trouble Songs without "trouble," we ought to linger on "Trouble" Songs without trouble. There is the possibility that something more than ineffectiveness[1] is at stake in the "Trouble" Song. That is to say, there may be an absence in presence to counterpoint the presence in absence of the singer's "trouble" gesture spoken of in other modules.[2]

Before we proceed, let's acknowledge (again?) that "Part Two" is a cipher. The reader is free and encouraged to read as she may, glean and skim and skip around, as the rear-view ever allows. So why Part Two? To let the sun shine in.[3] To continue in text along

---

1   and/or disaffection
2   This is a perhaps stilted avoidance of "earlier chapters," but it brings up another distinction at an opportune time. Module suggests on the one hand interchangeability, and on the other, mobility and self-containment. Just so, a song has a history and a relation to other songs, to other singers, while rooting itself in its passage. And then again, passage suggests history, transport, and instantiation. Let's not have indistinguishable pieces, but let's let them lie where we lay them, only to be picked up and replaced. Again, just so, the song is replaced by subsequent versions, and a 7″ can follow a CD. Which is (also) to say that we can play Cat Power's "[Satisfaction],"[a] then The Rolling Stones' "Satisfaction," and for us, this time, Cat Power comes first. If we work in modules, can we talk about what already happened, or should we bother? (And, then, why say "Part Two"?) We certainly ought to avoid repeating ourselves, if instead we can literally reiterate, replace repetition with re-placement.
    a   Let's say it this way, since Chan Marshall doesn't say it ("satisfaction") at all.
3   As "Trouble in Mind" has it, *the sun's gonna shine in my back door someday* (see "The Secret Rider" chapter — let's let this term, *chapter*, (back) in, now that we've troubled it).

the flow of readership and time. And, yes, there's a compiler here as well. The self that selves this might release himself, but he was here. There is a place and there is this place and there is the line let out. *I am just a dreamer / But you are just a dream,* sings Neil Young in "Like a Hurricane," and he's right,[4] and so are we — all of us blown away. Flit around, come back, and never read this again. *Insist on your freedom,* as Jack Kerouac didn't quite say.

---

4   even if you and I are confused

"Summer Days," Bob Dylan

She said, "You can't repeat the past." I said, "You can't? What do you mean you can't? Of course you can."

Who said that? Dylan? Someone he was talking to? MacDonald Carey and Alan Ladd in *The Great Gatsby*? Someone in a novel?

We repeat ourselves all the time in conversation, sometimes in print. We repeat each other more often in print. When we sing, we sing each other's lines. When we talk about trouble, we say it or we don't say it, and when we listen, we want it to go away, or we want to know it's there. So there's solace in Trouble Song, whether it's a summoning or a dispersal.[5] To the extent that trouble is here in song, we feel safe. To the extent it hasn't been allowed in, we fear its encroachment. Or we're superstitious, we want to have a good time, and we rely on irony to deliver us from what's at stake. We light our cigarettes on the fire, look up, and smell our soles.

Trouble is elusive, of course. Of course, along the way, trouble is down the line, on the way, follows us out the door. If we invite the possibility that "trouble" can replace trouble, the "Trouble" Song must already exist. At some limit of (de)stability, this song readmits trouble, as a shy dog taunted turns vicious, or Bloody Mary replaces your face after enough revolutions of the knife in the mirror.[6] For now, let's bar the door. "Trouble" Song is to be distinguished from Trouble Song. The former is a chant without a reference, a wolfen mascot with foam teeth that houses a vicious boy with an all-American smile. This is trouble-en-abyme, a baby swallowing a nested doll. Try as we might to evacuate the song, to neutralize "trouble," it grows grotesque in echo. Which is not to say the "Trouble" Song does not (cannot) exist. We must pursue it further into the surface of the song.

---

5 the relief promised in sharing a burden
6 *Speak my name and I appear,* Joanna Newsom sings like or as Bloody Mary in "Easy" — or she entreats us to call her, if not by her own name.

You Know That I'm No Good — Amy Winehouse & the Trouble Barrier

Or, The Semipermeable :Trouble: Membrane

How long is the lifespan of someone who grows up in public? Winehouse died at 27, a luckless seven years after her debut album, *Frank,* turned eyes and ears on Amy. As a child actor, she was not unaccustomed to attention. *Frank* reintroduced an enormously talented, anachronistic vocalist who belted and cinched her own material, and assured all mics that she had more to give. She backed it up with 2006's *Back to Black,* as she reached beyond *Frank*'s jazzy frame, embracing r&b, soul, ska, and '60s girl-group pop. Damn. And damned by her own hand — she wove and wavered stories of dissolution and ache, popping her eyes under flared eyeshadow that obviated an eyetooth wink.

On July 23, 2011, sighs were mixed with flip *are you surprised* comments in the culture web, as her media carcass was sewn up for the day. Details would be forthcoming, but the judgment had been cast years ago: another cracked doll for fame to toss onto the pyre.

But a funny thing happened to anyone who put the music on again. It sounded 50 years old and right now, not always in the same song.[7] A few days later, it sounded back from the pyre, side two to *Phases and Stages*'[8] side one: at turns degraded and destroyed, and back in the game. Climbing out of the whole mess. The strength of her voice became re-apparent. She sounded alive. Proud, in pain, alive. Broken, alive. Once again, her voice the best rebuttal to the worst footage of her we could find. The

---

7   To listen to her B-side cover of Phil Spector's "To Know Him Is to Love Him" is to *know, know, know* and lose time and place; to hear "Rehab" is to nod *no, no, no* in 2006. To know and not know, to no — this is trouble, with Amy Winehouse.

8   Willie Nelson's 1974 broke-up-and-get-it-together concept album breaks it down side-to-side.

candor of her music made us fresh — who were we to think she wanted us to know her?

Here, we have her at her best, so overfull and leaning in we know there's more.[9] Now, *Back to Black* is another old soul record — we can't believe it ever ends.

---

[9] The B-side "Valerie" is the crook-fingered siren calling us to the vault; we barely register the rattlesnake warning at the end of the track.

Trouble With History

> *History is hysterical: it is constituted only if we consider it, only if we look at it — and in order to look at it, we must be excluded from it.*
> — Roland Barthes, *Camera Lucida*

For Barthes, here, history is transported, or perhaps replaced, by a photograph of his mother. The photograph — and its version of history — excludes him not (only) because he is not in it, or because his mother is dead, but because he does not remember her outfit. It is clothing before him. His mother in the photo cannot conceive of him.

Does the song know we are there? Does trouble recognize us, or merely occupy our minds? Can we conceive of a song without hearing it in our heads? There is no trouble that is not called. Awareness is existence. *No troubles* is a negative value positively rendered. It is equal to *Trouble, trouble, I've had it all my days,* just as *They'll wash your troubles, your troubles, your troubles away* is an accumulation. Trouble is history, and history is hysterical. The borrowed song is evidence of our nonexistence. The song comes before us, carries past us. We sound out trouble as we take it in. We absorb the sign of our absence, asserting ourselves as such. *I'm not there* is also a negative value positively rendered.

This is the trick of history, the illusion of historicization. *Not there* is not here. To historicize is to assert that one exists — an hysterical claim. The Trouble Song sings trouble away, then, as it sings before the self. Rather than sing the song here, the singing I transports itself to the song. *No troubles,* no self, and vice versa.

So the Trouble Song without "trouble" is a wish fulfilled, already happened. The "Trouble" Song is neutered, or imagines itself so. This is the lie of the present: Now is neutral, a free wheel between past and future. If the "Trouble" Song is demystified language, all surface, the broken spell, it is a reassertion of (it) self. It is a pathetic *I was there* that trades the past for the present, or puts the present away. It is the failed cover, the thin wrap under which the self appears to gleam. It is a false preservation.

It is a desperate attempt at meaninglessness, a willful forgetting. The Trouble Song makes the singer disappear; the "Trouble" Song makes the song disappear. Neither succeeds in making trouble go away.

Trouble is not the word, it is the singing. Unspoken language has no magic. Speech cannot act without us, but words can make us disappear. *I was there* is a sleight of hand that reveals *But now I'm gone*. In *Nausea,* Sartre is translated by memory: *The record is scratched; perhaps the singer is dead.* If Gil Scott-Heron has died, have your troubles, your troubles, your troubles washed away?

"You Can't Put Your Arms Around a Memory"

1978. Or now. When is now? The song says here is what is gone, means the opposite of what it says, or says the opposite of what is says. Or it does the opposite of what it asserts. Always did, and certainly does now. Perhaps the song did not achieve its end until Johnny Thunders did the inevitable, and went the way of the singer, if not (always) the song.

All the smart boys know why. In the first chorus, we aren't sure whether he means it until he says *Don't try.* He doesn't need to say it again, or we don't need him to, but we're grateful for it when he does.

"Can't Keep My Eyes on You" is the fair-haired sister to this thought.

If you shouldn't try, you shouldn't cry. No, these are two imperatives, unrelated. The singer willfully misinterprets these tears, which are not in frustration, not a failed attempt to substantiate memory, to reach for what is not there. They are perhaps tears that acknowledge what the singer knows, that the singer can only know: the singer cannot hear the song. But he can see the tear on the face of the listener, the opening magnified by a drop, the fracture, the loss. The singer can always see the loss. He sings it back, to lose it again.

"Can't Keep My Eyes on You" is an answer song, an assertion, a manic *Don't try,* or a *Can't try,* or a *Why try?* There's nothing to cry about here, or *Don't cry* carries an exclamation. This is the flipside to all the smart boys know. It's *You know I'm true* vs. *You know it's true.*

Trouble is unspoken, or unspeakable, or unconveyable. You can't put your arms around it, except that in speaking it, if you can manage to speak it, it's the most obvious fact in the world. Trouble is self-generating, but it's also self-negating. To speak trouble is to lose it. Trouble is "Can't Put Your Arms Around a Memory" and "Can't Keep My Eyes on You." It is not-there in its presence. The spoken thing away. The genius[10] in a bottle.

---

10 and genus, and genre, and spirit, and the de-spirited

The Secret Rider

Perhaps we carry trouble of which we are unaware. A repressed anxiety, forgotten debt, secret rider, death's envoy. An old record absorbed as a gift. Someone else's father, the father of a friend, a strange father, perhaps an uncle, plays along with "Trouble in Mind." Credited here to Bobby Blue, this countrified blues standard is the last track on Asleep at the Wheel's *Texas Gold* (1975), whose cover image is a reverie on the text-masking from Neil Young's *After the Gold Rush*. This "Trouble in Mind," like numerous versions of Richard M. Jones's 1924 composition, assures itself, through vicissitudes and permutations,[11] that *the sun's gonna shine in my back door someday*.

As ever, there's a dusky comfort to the line. The sun doesn't yet shine through the blue house. Anyway, it's the singer who is blue, though he makes room for this confusion. The sun will shine in his back door, and take his blue mind away. Will he be facing that back door, gazing at what's gone, when that sun rises? Will he see it over his shoulder?[12] Or will it sneak up on his ass? Perhaps this is a vision of trouble catching up to him, the last light we wish to escape. If we don't believe him, it's because we know trouble won't leave us alone with our thoughts for long. We're more convinced the 219 train[13] can pacify[14] the singer's mind, as he lays his head on the lonesome lines of his false, jovial song.

---

11 Dylan borrows the title and rewrites the song. His version appears as the B-side to 1979's "Gotta Serve Somebody," the lead-off single from his born-again *Slow Train Coming*. If trouble is a death's head in the back of the mind, Dylan's A-side, with its concession, *It may be the devil,* is the service announcement that sets trouble aside for a moment.

12 *Ask Lot what he thought when his wife turned to stone,* Dylan offers (and commands) in his version. He skips the sunshine in the back door, still warning: *Dont look back* (as ever, he leaves the apostrophe behind, or leaves behind the apostrophe, taking it with him on his way out).

13 or 2:19 — time or number, it will surely come

14 or *ease* (Ella Fitzgerald, Dinah Washington, Jerry Lee Lewis, Johnny Cash et al.), or *satisfy* (Lightnin Hopkins), as other versions have it

The song is scratched on the record, caught in the throat. *The record is scratched; perhaps the singer is dead.*[15] To sing trouble is to sing with the voice of the dead, to voice the death the singer carries. If the singer takes the song, as Johnny Cash does, as Chan Marshall and Bob Dylan do, he takes death as well. He does not sing the song alive, nor does he revive the dead singer. He becomes the dead singer, his own. It is a version of death that he sings. And all who hear, hear their own death.

After all, "Trouble in Mind" is a suicide song, a self-negating comedy. The singer reports his own death, sings himself away in each verse, laughing to keep from crying. It's the last song he'll ever sing, and if you buy him another round, he'll sing it again: *'Cause I know the sun's gonna shine in my back door someday.* If the trouble, the blues, is in his mind, and the sun can take it away, can light up the blue, it needs a way in. This is the singer's secret rider, his clause: The microphone is a weapon pointed not at the audience, but at himself. He exhales death, but there's a report through the back of his skull, letting the sun shine in.[16]

Is, then, *I won't be blue always* a promise or a threat? Once we hear the threat in the promise (*I feel like I could die*),[17] it's all the same. *If the blues don't leave me...*[18]

---

15 to make a refrain of Sartre's *Nausea*
16 Dylan's version reads what he leaves out, talking to the other side and concluding:
    Satan will give you a little taste, then he'll move in with rapid speed,
    Lord keep my blind side covered and see that I don't bleed.
17 Johnny Cash prefaces the line with *Life ain't worth livin*
18 which Nina Simone follows with *If the Lord don't help me*

Not Wanting to Listen to Trouble Songs, Refrain

> *As counterpoise to a purity that found its bearings in disillusioned sadness, it is the "poetic" unsettlement of analytic utterance that testifies to its closeness to, cohabitation with, and "knowledge" of abjection.*
> — Julia Kristeva, *Powers of Horror*

The Trouble Song is reckless comfort to the singer, and to the listener. We are attracted to trouble, compelled to sing its name. And attraction carries the germ of repulsion, as ever. We'd rather face the singer, sing the song, than approach trouble directly. But that bravery — contingent, buffered, abstracted — is nonetheless a demand. It is also a command, a summons. Some (part) of us resist(s) that call. This comes from the awareness, or the suspicion, that "trouble" is trouble. That thrill of fear is integral to the appeal,[19] and carries its[20] germ.

We do not object to the Trouble Song, but we may abject (to) it, as we allow it to objectify trouble. If we cannot make trouble leave us, we can defy it, capture it, even celebrate it for the length of a song. We make ourselves listen (/sing). We purge trouble in this way, but we get ahead of ourselves. Why objectify trouble at all? Why not avoid it altogether? Reject it by not singing/listening. The flaw in the gem of this logic is the germ of the system. Trouble is our condition. It does not exist only because we name it. Just so, we forget death until our next (phlegmatic) cough.[21] Death is the great troubling of life. It is the rattle in the voice which makes the song catch. (Return to previous two footnotes — cough cough.) Death is the only escape from trouble. And it is the escape into trouble. And it (death, trouble) lingers in the song. Trouble is death, and not more than death, but also other than death. The awareness of death provokes the abject response: nausea in all its extents, greater and lesser. The Trouble

---

19 the appeal that is an offer, a supplication, as well as a draw
20 fear's, appeal's, fear's appeal
21 The song, then, is a clearing of the throat, and a sign that all songs will end.

Song is a lesser extent. The singer brings forth words, not bile. Or words, bilious, in stead of bile.

Abjection can be felt but not known, for it is an experience of death, or like unto the experience of death, which the living cannot carry.[22] Trouble, in its guise as impossible or nonperformative speech, has a similar operation. By nonperformative, we must distinguish between the linguistic coverage of the sign and its distance from — and replacement for — the referent: "trouble" but not trouble. The call that is a refusal to call.[23] "Trouble" is a refrain, in all ways. In the Trouble Song, it[24] may be felt because it may not be known.

The living cannot abide (in) death, must abject (to) it. The singer/listener can hear "trouble," but does not wish to listen to what it says.[25] *It* is the song, *it* is the singer/listener. Abjection comes with the collapse of the subject/object distinction. Neither can the singer/listener[26] bear trouble; so she surrenders to objectification. The song is losing oneself/itself, which is to be desired and feared. The lesser loss, momentary, is sought, to forestall awareness of the greater loss, in eternity. The trouble that, rather than going away, takes her away.

---

22 or inhabit
23 or calls the refusal to answer
24 trouble
25 After all, "trouble" says trouble, in stead of trouble. To hear is to replace: signification as signification, a process to replace its end and its origin.
26 another collapse

The Trouble With Superman

A whole lotta trouble is called out in the first lines of "The Man of METROPOLIS Steals Our Hearts," as Sufjan Stevens references the unmentionable American product. The Superman clip-art cover of *Illinois*[27] invites copyright trouble and is covered by a John Wayne Gacy-riffing balloons sticker,[28] which makes the composition more and less coherent.[29] It also reiterates another kind of trouble,[30] this one absorbed by the album (whereas Superman himself[31] is externalized[32] to different effect).[33] Meanwhile, in a related concern, cultural priorities (molestation vs. fair use/copyright) are exercised/abused, and Stevens's 50-albums-for-50-states ambition invites future trouble — a curse like "trouble," the curse of attention, pressure, doubt, process, tedium. If it's a gag, it's a controlling one: Stevens will be known as the guy who claimed he was making a 50-album concept album, whether or not he makes another installment in the series (and/or for as long as we have to wait for another city to burst into songs). On the other hand (the one that just held a bunch of balloons), to say *I'm making 50 albums, one for each state* is a

---

27 AKA *Illinoise*, AKA *Come on Feel the Illinoise*
28 on the early vinyl edition: three balloons, to carry three troubles (two "troubled," one "trouble") in the first two lines of the "title" song; any one balloon might reference the lure of the child murderer in Fritz Lang's 1931 film *M* (fka *Mörder unter uns*, or *Murderer Among Us*, or more to the point, as the title was an implicit critique of the Nazi rise to power in Germany, *The Murderers Are Among Us*)
29 The original cover collages Illinois-ing images of the Chicago metropolis skyline, over which Superman soars, with a quartet of UFOs, a goat, and Al Capone. The Superman-UFO vector is science-fictional, while Superman and Capone pair as good-guy/bad-guy antagonists. The balloons foreground the album's Gacy motif, drawing Capone's bemused attention while erasing Superman from the equation — though they do so conspicuously, a chalkboard erasure that leaves a ghost image. The cursed goat (which foiled the Chicago Cubs) stands out to the side.
30 reference trouble
31 or "Superman" itself
32 or exiled
33 he/it is sublimated, or "sublimated" — we know he's (not) there

species of speech act (and pipe dream) relatable to the claim that "trouble" might displace trouble.

The song stands for the album in a more and less visible way. It opens side three with Superman's "appearance," a moment when he flies from the literal cover-art cityscape to the implied lyrical universe of the album. However, due to the machinations of copyright, he leaves the cover (or is obscured by balloons)[34] and can only be referred to (and not named) in the song. Even before trouble arrives over the image, he is not named, but rather cloaked in "Man of Steel," in which he is recast as *only a steel man*. Either way, we see him clearly enough, even if our gaze can't penetrate the balloon sticker that throws off all scale.[35]

Stevens's stated[36] project, to cover all 50 states in a series of themed albums, was awe-inspiring and doomed[37] as mere ambition from the start. As whisper-sung hubris, it is impeccable: to

---

34 which gives way in other editions to a balloonless and Supermanless sky, and a fourth version in which the balloons sink into the surface, or everything rises to meet them

35 cultural, compositional, parallactical: Either the obscured Superman is far enough away to fit behind the balloons, or the balloons are nearby, as though the adjacent Al Capone, standing in for John Wayne Gacy, has just released them. But they drift toward him, strings streaming away. Perhaps the wind has shifted, just as his cigar-chomping grin seems more appropriate now that Superman isn't coming for him — or has The Man of Steel merely disguised himself as a snare of balloons? Will Gacy-clowning-as-Capone (and/or Peter Lorre) be entangled in his own inconography? Has Stevens effectively deflected the danger in his material? Or has he stepped into it, putting on his "John Wayne Gacy, Jr." robe (or clown suit) of song, crooning

    ... in my best behavior
    I am really just like him
    Look beneath the floorboards
    For the secrets I have hid

Here, let the sticker be the floorboard, let the market of images be his field of prey.

36 or advertised; and who takes an advertisement for its word, or for more than its words?

37 Chicagoan rock writer Jessica Hopper's *The First Collection of Criticism by a Living Female Rock Critic* (2015) includes an open letter to Stevens from her 2006 *Village Voice* Pazz & Jop Critics Poll dispatch in which she invites him to go for a drive through Chicago to visit some of the local gems he missed

say *50 albums, one for each state* is to make room for them in the imagination. To provide a sample like *Michigan* and *Come on Feel the Illiniose* is to prove the phenomenon as immanence[38] if not imminence. Stevens's own well-publicized Christianity underwrites a faith in great endeavor, if not (earthly) reward; his soft-spoken delivery and dewy visage disarm his own immodesty.

So industry replaces heroism in the song's topography, and the stealing cover becomes steel-driven popcraft. And the legend of Sufjan Stevens sings itself.[39]

---

    in his catalog, including an industrial dumping ground, the disused atrium of the Harold Washington Library, and a vegan soul food restaurant.

38 the sharing of which — among listeners who can imagine the complete set — is faith

39 just as Stevens, who holds a creative writing MFA from The New School — inflates, animates and conflates fiction and nonfiction (and popcraft) in song

Trouble Returns

"The modern style of interpretation excavates, and as it excavates, destroys; it digs 'behind' the text, to find a sub-text which is the true one" (Sontag, *Against Interpretation* 6). The Trouble Song, as passed from mouth to ear, resists hermeneutic reconstruction in that it presents a signifier that is also signified. The Trouble Song, as handed along, refers to itself, but also allows the listener to sing it her own way, to compound the reference. Again, *Whose trouble?* And an answer: *Yours and mine.* That is perhaps to say the singing/hearing is itself an interpretive gesture, if not a cooperative one. The listener wants what the singer does not have,[40] whether it is access to the content of "troubles," or the remedy for trouble. Simultaneously, the song is analgesic, a buffer. Its refusal to signify outside of itself, its insistence on transmitting itself rather than presenting trouble,[41] suspends pain, keeps trouble at the door by inviting it to stay[42] awhile. Trouble, like the Trouble Song, is always already (t)here, and to call it is to attempt to summon a permeable sphere of reference. "Trouble" may in this sphere be inhabited by multiple spirits, corporeal and referential,[43] that come and go as they please.

---

40 and/or cannot (or will not) offer

41 or presenting trouble (a generality) instead of (particular) troubles, "trouble" instead of trouble

42 Here we take advantage of multiple inflections of *stay,* so trouble is made (or beseeched) to remain put. We can take its power by evoking it, though we risk an overstay of its (un)welcome. Trouble can outwait the song, step outside of it, or step into it as the (reckless/unruly) singer. The alliance between listener and singer can thus be broken, or put in radical flux. Fragmentation can occur among performer and audience, or between singer-as-singer and singer-as-listener. In the latter case, the collapse of categories paradoxically allows trouble to become a force that moves through the singer, and may as well possess as control him: at least three covalent entities (singer and song; song and trouble; singer and trouble) in differentiable, chaotically modal relations. Nor is the performer the only singer in the room.

43 The more interpretations the song allows, the safer the singer/listener is from harm (from the trouble "behind" "trouble"). Trouble is dispersed by the collaborative open reference of "trouble." *Whose trouble? Ours.* The ambiguity of this trouble — that it may be a shared singular and specific trou-

The song gets its charge by allowing this proximity while maintaining semantic and interpersonal distance.[44] Each player decides — or has the illusion of deciding — on her level of intimacy with trouble and its representations. If all players carry trouble, and may come and go, so might trouble(s) appear to disappear.

---

ble, or may be a generally acknowledged collection of trouble (*we all have troubles of our own*) — is essential to the voyeuristic and heuristic promises/premise(s) of the song.

44 This is to say, the presence of the particular audience contributes to the meaning of a particular song performance. The song is in this sense a collaboration between all present (and/with previous singer/audiences). It is both representation and presentation, in that a familiar song may be repeated, (but) is/as a unique, non-reproducible event.

Lost in the Paradise

My little grasshopper airplane cannot fly very high

Sometimes a penis is just a penis. Sometimes its name is green wave death. Caetano Veloso, who found "Lost in the Paradise," and Gal Costa, who found it again — each borrows its troubles and hides their name. Veloso is credited as the songwriter, but this is not a written song:

> *I am the sun, the darkness*
> *My name is green wave*
> *Death, salt, South America is my name*
> *World is my name, my size*
> *And under my name here am I*

These are impossible claims, inscrutable demands. This verse is the perfect alibi, which can be repeated but not discovered. To say *South America is my name* is to refuse name and place. In Veloso's version, *My name is green wave death* is the punchline, the villain's confession that says goodbye, admits everything: *You are dead, and I am yours.* Which is to say: *I am your killer.* Who can claim to be nature?

Also in 1969, John Barth's fifth book, *Lost in the Funhouse*, was published. The title story begins: "For whom is the funhouse fun? Perhaps for lovers." Veloso's song, "Lost in the Paradise," begins with a similar diffuse warning: *My little grasshopper airplane cannot fly very high*. As Costa sings it, the drama is the withholding of the name, while Veloso builds to the delivery, the fecund gift of death.

The typical male orgasm carries hundreds of thousands of deaths, and perhaps one death-in-life, one suspended sentence. *My name is green wave death* is that death sentence which refuses to be a refrain, unless the song is repeated, by the listener or the singer, or by another singer. It happens once, forever. It is the dead sister to *My little grasshopper airplane cannot fly very high*. The latter is clear-spoken in Costa's "Lost in the Paradise";

the former is lost in the funhouse of the song, a staccato secret buried in the noir shadows of her version.

What's the trouble with "Lost in the Paradise"? Must we say it? Can we not pass [through] the distorting mirror and leave it alone, or does our image stick, grotesque and forlorn and marked for death? The song is a photo, of the singer and her object, and of the listener:

Don't help me, my love
My brother, my girl
Just tell my name
Just let me say who am I

These lines were written by Veloso. They are writeable, and speakable, and therefore repeatable. The song slows down to accept them, even as *My brother, my girl* is irreconcileable, an invitation to Costa to help deliver the message. *My name is green wave death* may not be said again. The trouble with "Lost in the Paradise" begins with the impotence of its opening lines — *My little grasshopper airplane cannot fly very high.*[45] In time, it passes through the impossible confession at its heart: *My name is green wave death.* Reader, we have done the impossible. We have repeated the unrepeatable. May trouble spare us all.

---

45 The line is unspeakable, *anymore* is unspoken.

Enter Trouble America

In "The Public Relation: Redefining Citizenship By Poetic Means," Erín Moure explores the notion of citizenship as movement, which she describes as "the troubled and transgressive relation of this citizen to borders" (*My Beloved Wager* 167). So might a Trouble Song[46] be a moving [through] place. In the same essay, she makes reference to "troubled text" (163). "It is as if site or country itself were performative or gestural, having more to do with languages than with soil" (168). Not, then, a song of country, nor even a country of song; not a country song, but perhaps a country-song (or country — song, or country : song).[47] If the country (say, The United States of America, if not Moure's native[48] Canada) is troubled territory, or, if we will, a troubled text, we might enter that terrain through the Trouble Song, and know (or recognize) ourselves (even and especially as others) there. We might hope to transgress our own borders as we pass through the song that has passed through the moving country.[49] We enter the blur of language that is The Trouble Song of America, and we sing (with) ourselves.

---

46 and/or a troubled song

47 Where the em-dash and colon operate as axes, around which the terms spin, tilling all terrain. As the song travels, or whirls, it also mulches the land, and the language. We hesitate, only briefly, to say/spread language. The em-dash also suggests a Deleuzian becoming, a line of flight between country and song, whose polarities may reverse or swivel.

48 an ever troubled term

49 history, but also a continuous present that is a line of flight to the future, whenever and wherever that is, which is to say *here* and *here* and *here* but also perhaps *there* &c.

Fugue on Anthology Minor

Or, Nobody Here but Us Ghosts

What are you looking for?

Don't say the word, we've already heard it.

You'd be the echo.

When you start coming after yourself…

Well then, what's the trouble?

The very word [the] is an ellipsis.

Some songs can't even say it.

The Anthology of American Folk Music, or *Smithsonian Folkways,* or *The Harry Smith Anthology.* Any way you call it, one man's records, or many people's records collected — captured — by one man. Seems like the whole chest, but even then, the coins were spilling out. Or — let's make it a coffin — here are *some of* the bodies.

Pity no one, really, can listen to the acetates. On headphones, the digital files carry static.

Resistance to *Social Music,* going on 13 years.[50] As if religion doesn't span the mass of them.[51]

All we have is introductions.[52] All we offer is same.

Totality vs. selection. *Who'll rock the cradle when I'm gone? I'll rock the cradle when you're gone.*

Drawn in & out. Drawn aside.

Thought: I can drink all night. This is history.

---

50 On a personal note: *Social Music,* Vol. Two of *The Anthology* would have pristine grooves, if the vinyl was available all those years ago, when I (at last the I reopens! — and inverts) picked up the Smithsonian CD set. In 2009, a three-volume vinyl edition was finally reissued. My first priority was obtaining Vol. Three, *Songs*. Next came Vol. One, *Ballads*. I have yet to pick up the Vol. 2 reissue.

51 *The Anthology* as a [riddled] whole is shot through with the power and fury of the Lord — God trouble. "Social Music" gathers spirituals and turn of the [19th-]century instrumental dance music. Perhaps an aversion to the tenor of this volume, rather than a secular bias, is cause for minimum rotation. As Greil Marcus sets the mood, "Smith's two lps of 'Social Music' are a respite, a place of simple pleasures where the most troubled heart is filled only with a gentle yearning" (*Invisible Republic* 107). If you're looking for trouble, you'll head for the outer volumes.

52 As Marcus describes in his indispensible "The Old, Weird America" chapter from *Invisible Republic* — so vital that a subsequent edition became *The Old Weird America,* and the eponymous chapter was included in the supplementary liner notes to the Smithsonian Anthology CD set, and Marcus taught an undergraduate lecture course at The New School about the folk lyric tradition under that name — Smith included a wealth of information, alchemically arranged, in his liner booklet. Along with the sharing and sequencing of his records, it is part of his contribution to (and gift of) the collection. More than that, it's a collaboration with the musicians whose performances are gathered here. It is just as deeply inscrutable, immediate, and troublesome as the music. It is a part of the music, and the booklet makes for transporting accompaniment to the records. And yet, it's another surface — a deep one. Just so, each song is a how-do-you-do from the beyond, even when the singer is talking to himself. As we listen, we respond in kind. *How do you do,* we sing along, with whatever words we find.

I wish I was a mole in the ground.

History as Harry Smith's record collection.

Yes I've been in the bin so long.

Some mistakes made to be made.

Know what I'm missing.

Yes I wish I was a mole in the ground.

Hear the material over the matter.

Or the matter over material — no difference.

Material : Matter

Well I didn't know you had any children.

Material song weather.

Material : Medium

No sir No sir No sir No sir

Did anyone say / Did anyone say that word

That word, you know.

I can't sleep for dreaming & I can't stay awake for

I wish my man

Did someone say

The word, you know.

Once you become your own echo…

Loneliness is the self-same chorus.

We don't know what trouble

But heard her sing

She's going where she please.

Can we tell

Can we tell these people

Can we tell these people are real?[53]

What they talk about in another language

That we recognize.

Cf. Sonny Boy Williamson, "Keep It to Yourself"

Trouble is what gets you.

---

[53] Yes, we should tell: These people are real. And so gone.

Occupied

Does trouble recognize us, or merely occupy our minds?[54]

Barthes' notion of hysterical history (applied) would suggest that we project ourselves onto/into trouble, leaving our selves behind. To which let's add that trouble is a story we tell to make ourselves (or, paradoxically, our troubles) disappear. As if the generic (and genre) will save us (or spare us, or spell us).

If [/as] we pass through the Trouble Song, we pass through trouble. Does the song know we are there? This depends on the nature of the audience. The singer is audience to the song, particularly the received Trouble Song. But if he plays to an expansive audience, we can imagine no individual comprises the audience, or the transmission. Does the singer recognize each [other] member of the audience? Not necessarily. Nor is it necessary for him to do so for trouble to be passed around. Does trouble know it is sung? What's the trouble.[55]

The Trouble Song lets us know trouble is there. It allows us to [safely] recognize trouble. It is a secure invitation. We [are allowed to] know trouble by its song. Let us ask again: Does trouble know us? If we are responsible for trouble, if we bring it to the table at the bar, does it rely on us?

We cannot know trouble, can only know its sign, under the Trouble Song. This is why the song is allowed into the party. We allow the song to get hold of us because we trust that trouble cannot keep us while we have an invocation to its double in play (the fake authentic jukebox at our table, both recalling and replacing the communal interface).

Does trouble recognize us? We hope not. We carry on under the disguise of revelry, or the pantomime of sentiment, the performance of trouble that keeps it at bay. We sing to have "trou-

---

54 Thanks to Chris Stroffolino for positing this question, regarding the Roland Barthes' epigraph from another Trouble Song ("Trouble With History"): "History is hysterical: it is constituted only if we consider it, only if we look at it — and in order to look at it, we must be excluded from it."
55 an answer in the form of a question, and vice versa

ble" in mind. If trouble remains anonymous, perhaps we can be anonymous to trouble.

Does trouble occupy our minds? In either form, in both: yes, but never merely so.

We Who Are [in] Trouble

Where are we in song? And who are we in song? When we listen, the song is set, even as the singer is free to adapt the song. The singer is a relational *I* — she is a mediated self affected by the song, the scene, the audience. The listeners are recognized as a *we* in this construction — as "listeners." The singer, however, is multiplied in the *I*-s of the listeners, becoming a *we*, just as the singer, in her awareness of other singers,[56] takes part in a WE bound by the song. The audience, conversely, is composed of relational *I*-s, an assembled *we*. This *we* is non-coercive because each listener shares "trouble," which may be personally identified[57] (or not) at will. This we borrows each one of us, under the name of the song, for its duration, and as Trouble Song. It is ours and belongs to none of us.

These are essential relations in the Trouble Song. Those songs that name trouble[58] may behave — or affect the singer/listener[59] — differently. They are not Trouble Songs, or they are another kind of trouble.

There is always another kind of trouble.

---

[56] Here we explicitly sing the cover, and/or the Trouble Song. The Trouble Song does not need to be a cover, except in the sense that any Trouble Song relates to Trouble (even if and as it only relates "trouble").

[57] if not articulated

[58] Perhaps *trouble* may be named, or is nameable, while *Trouble* may, and is, not — and perhaps only trouble at large (that is, Trouble) may be named.

[59] At the return of this figure — or this abstraction — let us re-emphasize the collapsing selves that comprise we-who-are-in-trouble, or We Who Are in Trouble Songs.

We Recruit(ed), We Reinscribe(d)

Do Trouble Songs recruit us? With what promises? *Trouble, no trouble, on the line.* See/return to "Trouble Returns." Or flip back to Side One (or, that is — or was — Part One). Then scratch out Part Two, call it Side Two.[60] Yes, let's call it Side Two, after we call it Side One.

---

60 Keeping Jonathan Lethem's calling-trouble in mind. In his 33 1/3 series monograph on Talking Heads' *Fear of Music*, he parses the difference between calling and naming, cf. "Heaven," as it is articulated (or not articulated) in the line *The name of the bar, the bar is called Heaven*. Which is to say, or not say, *The bar's* (if it is a bar, and not Heaven, or not (not) a place at all, or not a public place) *called Heaven* is not the same as *The bar's name is Heaven*. Whether David Byrne (or whoever he is in the song) has changed his mind and offered a pseudonym (for the bar), to throw us off or put us on, or whether he's trying to get it just right (whatever it is, whatever right is), might be up to us (whoever we are) to decide.

NY Trouble, World Trouble (Hidden Tracks)

On Saturday, August 25, 2012, the front page of *The New York Times* reports, "Gunman dies After Killing at Empire State Building": "The man, Jeffrey T. Johnson, lurked behind a van parked outside the drab office building that houses the apparel importer that had laid him off almost two years ago." Trouble abounds in today's *Times*. The left column at the head of the Arts & Leisure section is Melena Ryzik's ambivalent take on the cultural phenomenon of Pussy Riot, whose members are described as "well-accessorized Russian women" who present an "expertly constructed, perfectly charged" punk resurrection with "savvy reference to feminist and musical history — riot grrrl and Susie Bright, as well as a wink to women's appropriation of sexual agency and bodily power." After the jump to page 17, Ryzik quotes an email from Guerrilla Girls Kathe Kollwitz and Frida Kahlo: "Pussy Riot are our kind of girls: feminist activists in masks making trouble. ... The world needs more feminist masked avengers. We urge everyone to make trouble, each in her own way."

Below the fold, Chan Marshall (who sings trouble as Cat Power, even as her new album will let the *Sun* in) talks about Kanye West's post-Katrina salvo, *George Bush doesn't care about Black people,* from NBC's September 2, 2005 live broadcast of *A Concert for Hurricane Relief.*

Meanwhile, The Arts section runs a pull quote for writer Rachel Saltz's Fringe Festival theater review: "Trouble arrives when a daughter falls for a boy with a pulse." To the left of that piece is an interview with guitarist Ry Cooder, who has a new album called *Election Special*. The first page is "trouble" free, but after the jump, he's asked about his recent topical songs. He says, "If you don't have some creative outlet for yourself, I'm sorry, you're going to be in trouble, because there is so much that's coming."

On August 17, the day Maria Alyokhina, Yekaterina Samutsevich and Nadezhda Tolokonnikova are sentenced to two years in a penal colony, activists gather outside the Consulate General of the Russian Federation in New York to protest.[61] After police announce,[62] "You are being asked to remove your masks; if you do not, you will be arrested for loitering,"[63] they cuff, unmask, and lead at least two women to a paddy wagon. Among those who remain at relative liberty are a two-woman band with an acoustic guitar and a tambourine, who sing *You wanted trouble / We are the trouble / ... / You should be scared / It's just begun.*

---

61 as we observe from a window above
62 chanting into megaphones their promise-of-trouble song
63 for we know a loiterer by her mask, apparently

Part Three

TROUBLE ON THE LINE

I got so much trouble on my mind
Refuse to lose
Here's your ticket
— Public Enemy, "Welcome to the Terrordome"

Thanks for your time.
I don't have any time.
Thanks for your trouble then.
I don't have any trouble either.... nor do you, don't kid yourself.
— Pete Frame, Interview with Don Van Vliet, 1969

fuckflowers bloom in your mouth
will choke your troubles away
— Caroline Bergvall, *Goan Atom*

Take Apart: Room by Room

Not telling someone else's story: listening. Which is (a) taking part. Which is taking (a) part. Here's where I (and I-s) come in. What trouble have I? Only what I have reflected (on). We are and are not the same. Every self implies an other, and every other is a self. I am not you, but you are I. When we sing, when we are sung (to), we are the song. The song is (o)u*s[1] for its duration — takes our place. We tolerate trouble for that span. And more: We embrace trouble for a few minutes, then turn a side.

Right now on the hi-fi, spinning: Ann Peebles, *I Can't Stand the Rain*. How can we take part in what we take in? How can we get closer to a song that goes away? The needle spins into the record, away from us.[2] Into us, as we remove ourselves. The trouble is the record becomes us, but we do not impress the record.[3] There are other troubles, but this one bothers us even when the clouds go away. *I Can't Stand the Rain* is too short, not long enough, and perfect. Or just right, which has the limit perfection tosses off, repugnant. All she needs to do is repeat herself: *If we can't trust each other / We don't need one another*. All we need to do is listen — take part. Five more minutes would be too many, after all. We exit through the entrance (or enter the exit) of "One Way Street," *walking on troubled ground*.

---

1. That is, we own each other (our songs, ourselves), but not exclusively; still, we see the song as ourselves, which we pass on. *I'd like to buy the world a Coke and keep it company* is a sticky bottle of trouble in hand.
2. Meanwhile the record spins into the needle, tightening on the spindle.
3. Except as we wear the record down — a de-inscription.

Annie Clark, Becoming "Kerosene"[4]

Set me on fire. Or, "ST. VINCENT COVERS BIG BLACK at BOWERY BALLROOM NYC May 22 2011." As of April 6, 2013, the video registers 125,391 views on YouTube. Presumably, this represents at least 125,000 conflagrations. Annie Clark and her band set off through Big Black territory, covering not only the song, but perhaps the performance documented in another video on YouTube, "big black - kerosene."[5] *This is a song Jerry Lee Lewis wrote before he killed one of his wives,* Albini informs the crowd at the bottom of his breath, before he and his band angle into the performance. Albini appears to be covered in blood. His guitar is slung around his waist. Another guitarist walks in place as he carves out his part. Albini paces, hacking away at his dick. The bassist is all over the E string, winding the song.[6] The drummer punches his drums. *I was born in this town / Lived here my whole life / Probably come to die in this ____[7] / Lived here my whole life.* Ominous whine, murderous complaint. *There's kerosene around find something to do.*

Someone is on fire. Someone is set on fire. Annie Clark carries her guitar higher on her torso, high on her belly, at her solar plexus. It[8] is a shield, and it will become a badge. It is a shield for the song, shielding her from it. It is the shell of the song, encasing her. She is carving her stomach. She is scratching the chakra aligned with Survival Issues. Or it is Manipura, city of jewels, associated with dispelling of fear, and the power to destroy the world. Or create it. The solar plexus absorbs *prana,* or life, from the sun.[9]

---

[4] Thanks to participants in two New School Graduate Writing Program seminars, DEEP SURFACE (fall 2012) and MAKING TEXT (spring 2013) — two discussions covered in this version.

[5] 329,726 views

[6] or: The bassist marshals the E string, bearing the song.

[7] Here the "town" (if not the town) disappears.

[8] solar plexus, shield

[9] So says Wikipedia.

Annie Clark is ablaze. She shakes her head, Bill Pullman/Balthazar Getty's transformative Fred/Pete gesture in David Lynch's *Lost Highway*. Before this moment, Greil Marcus might say the band is looking for the song, or playing it. Then the song plays them. The band is aflame, whereas Big Black is merely on fire. The precedent is a pack of boys, and one boy on fire. The latter is the voice of Kerosene.

If in both versions, Kerosene is girl and fuel, and in the former version, the boy sets himself on fire, or sets upon Kerosene, the only thing to do in this town, as all the boys have learned,[10] St. Vincent is the apotheosis of Kerosene, not merely the living flame, but the singing flame. She is fire, is a flame, and as she touches the boys, she loses herself. This is her risk, her wager. Kerosene and the boys, the boy and the girl, becoming-flame. They consume themselves with otherness, and with the other.

The rest is two videos, a dancing pile of ash, flames in the eyes of the crowd.

---

10 as all the boys have taught her

If I Stay Here, Trouble Will Find Me[11]

> *Renfield says to Harker concerning the latter's forthcoming trip to Transylvania: "And, young as you are, what matters if it costs you some pain — or even a little blood?" A warning that occults the real danger, even when it seems a prophesy revealing the worst that can happen. It is exactly when the character has a hint that something so terrible that it goes beyond anything he could have expected (or can expect) may soon happen to him that he tells himself If only I had listened then, precisely not to heed what the present situation should disclose to him: that the warning was misleading since it says that the worst that can happen is that he will lose a little blood, or even, since one can negotiate how little is little, that he will die from losing too much blood. The warning hides that the danger is not the cessation of life but madness and undeath; hence it was an exaggeration hiding from him that no exaggeration could disclose the danger threatening him.*
> — Jalal Toufic, *(Vampires)*

I was afraid / I'd eat your brains leads, naturally,[12] to *I'm evil*. Or, more properly,[13] vice versa. On record,[14] it sounds mock-gothic, a light moment[15] for a heart of darkness. *Cuz I-I-I'm eeevil*. Live, it implicates the crowd, which moans along, barks at the moon. An army of the undead.[16]

Pittsburgh, Stage AE.[17] June 11, 2013. The National is touring for *Trouble Will Find Me*, dipping into its previous release. Matt Berninger paces the stage like a less disheveled Professor Mark

---

11 Or Trouble, With White Girls; Or Jenny Jenny I'm Seeing Double
12 or, as it were, un-naturally
13 or, as it may be, logically
14 *High Violet* (2010), by The National
15 and, perhaps, a leitmotif
16 whether they are self-aware zombies in (Romero's) Pittsburgh, or bleeding-heart vampires in The National's own Brooklyn backyard
17 that is, American Eagle's stage; just past PNC (Bank) Stadium, where real-life Pittsburgh pirates take the streets for a Bucs game

E. Smith,[18] heading stage left, then changing his mind, and direction, etc. *Oh, there's my water, then.* It's feelingly contrived, a necessary pose.[19] Later, after he has stalked through the crowd, roadies and techs holding the endless microphone cable aloft, and again stands, a bit more disheveled now, he will compulsively pour his heretofore charmed water[20] on the stage, then spike the cup. He will then confess, as stage hands clean up after him, *That was my fault, an accident.*

"Trouble" finds two songs on the following album.[21] One verse[22] begins,[23] *Jenny I'm having trouble* and goes on to confess *Jenny I'm seeing double* just as Jenny is doubled in sound and vision.[24] In another song,[25] *I was a white girl in a crowd of white girls in a park.* The trouble with white girls is apparently not only in telling them apart, but in telling oneself apart from them.[26] In

---

18 another distinction in his general bearing being that he does not put the band through its paces, rather seems to indulge himself in its ambient embrace (or embrace himself in its ambience)
19 or sequence (of poses)
20 that is, ever-flowing
21 *Trouble Will Find Me* (2013)
22 or is it a chorus?
23 or continues
24 all of this moments before the leap between records one and two of the gatefold vinyl
25 a Trouble Song without "trouble"
26 Here as elsewhere, The National cites its own lyrical universe (just as its sonics are instantly recognizable, and it can be difficult to remember, if one cares to, on which album a particular song resides), portalled as it is to the one we share. Or here again is where The National revises or re-versions its script. *I was a white girl in a crowd of white girls in a park* ("Pink Rabbits") is a brother to a sister to *I used to be / carried in the arms of cheerleaders / I'm the new blue blood / I'm the great white hope* ("Mr. November") and *I'm a birthday candle in a circle of Black girls* ("All the Wine"). In each case a limit is tested and buttons are more or less gently pushed. The singer/speaker is audibly masculine and male, but makes claims to (and (up)on) femininity and the female (generalizations are inevitable here, and are very much in play). All this is built on a house of race cards. There's always a crowd of girls (public or intimate), and an I is always there, only apparently with (or without) a fixed gender or race. All of these lyrics are problematic, but are they belligerent or marginalizing, and who is subject and object in these

sympathy, the album is full of other people's troubles,[27] like "Sea of Love," an original with a cover for a title, a "Hey Joe" refrain, and the sense to realize *If I stay here / Trouble will find me*[28] and/ or *If I stay here / I'll never leave*. On an album that admits *If you want / to see me cry / Play Let It Be / or Nevermind* and *I wish that I could rise above*,[29] contamination anxiety is not the trouble, though trouble is invited.[30]

Meanwhile, and all the while, the Crescendo Twins Dessner[31] hold up the sky.[32] Since Berninger, in a band of musical overachievers, does no more than sing, one assumes he provides all vocals. The show puts the lie to this view, as there are backing vox all around — most prominently, and cherub-like, from the twins.[33]

---

constructions? In any case, they are entitled lyrics, even lyrics of entitlement, but they are also lyrics about entitlement. (Here we recall an argument for Flarf Poetry's remix of problematic language: It's not racist/sexist/homophobic, it's *about* racism/sexism/homophobia. It's not simply enacting or reinscribing problematic language, but criticizing or recasting it. Thus we are, presumably, prepared for (and provoked to) critical discourse, or at least self/other-awareness.) Whether or not they are sexist or racist, they at least insinuate they are about sex, gender and race, or they engage our feelings about them. Songs are about feeling, whether it's on display in the song, or it's primarily generated or evoked in the listener. Perhaps the more appropriate question here is not *What's the trouble?* but *Who's (in) trouble?*

[27] or other people's Trouble Songs

[28] Line break indications added to indicate pauses in cadence (if not visible caesura): appropriately, the lyrics are printed in unlineated blocks on the slip cases. Even after multiple listens, Berninger's well-placed breaths are inscrutable.

[29] or, perhaps, *I wish that I could Rise Above*, as Berninger suggests in the moments he screams like Rollins (or Black Francis) over the mic

[30] All the white girls in the house say *yeah!*

[31] Aaron and Bryce, who wave the black flag Carl Wilson burns in his Slate piece "Why I Hate the National," as he compares their band to the "Crescendo Rock" of U2, Radiohead and, ouch, Coldplay (for whom Wilson may harbor a bit of pity for its (unlikely) underdog status).

[32] though nothing they can do — and they do a lot — can do anything but bring down this guy, though magestically so

[33] or, admittedly, from one or the other of them

If only I had listened then is our refrain, as trouble comes knocking, and as we trip over the floor at the door.[34] Or, as we recall the easy invitation we gave: Trouble, come on in. We danced, we sang along — *I'm evil!* — and we were forever without end roped in.

---

[34] Toufic distinguishes between the *false threshold* and the threshold itself, though our recognition of the *false threshold* might not help us, as he coins it, since it may in actuality be our last chance to turn away from The Castle, from The Count. After that, we're (always) already in.

Trouble Will Find You[35]

1, 2

Trouble, trouble, I've had it all my days   Trouble with a capital T   Trouble with people like me   Trouble, trouble, it seems like trouble going to follow me to my grave   She was drinking down her troubles   Have trouble at my door   Troubles, no troubles, on the line   They'll wash your troubles, your troubles, your troubles away   In that troubled water   Trails of troubles   When I've got trouble even opening a honey jar   I told you I was trouble   Trouble in mind, I'm blue   Trouble falls in my home   Troubled man, troubled stone   You wanted trouble   We are the trouble

3

Ain't that asking for trouble   Have you ever been in trouble   Trouble ahead, trouble behind   Everyone around me knows I'm in trouble   Because I've got troubles enough   He never took much trouble   Don't it make your troubles seem small   They tell me when you tell somebody your troubles   Trouble fly away from you   Then when you're just about to doze, fly trouble   And there was trouble, taking place   I got girl trouble up the ass   I thought about trouble trouble   Where's my little trouble girl?   We would stay out of trouble   If you decide to make me blue, I'll be in trouble   So I just want you to know, I'll be in trouble   You're in love and I'm in trouble   Keep smiling at trouble 'cause trouble is a bubble   Little trouble girl   Well,

---

35   In which Trouble Songs come home to roost: a nest of lines culled from songs referenced in parts one and two, and from an ongoing list of Trouble Songs compiled from research and suggestions. This methodological bump of the turntable is offered instead of a complete, ordered list of lines from songs referenced throughout the book, as that would suggest a sense of order and completion that runs counter to the project. We humbly offer this as the "Trouble Songs" to replace Trouble Songs.

this trouble in the house   Trouble on the stairs   Trouble in the trouble   That trouble in the air   Nobody knows the trouble I've seen   We don't need no more trouble   Tiny bubbles are always leadin' me knee deep into some sort of trouble   Wisdom forgot them so they became trouble   So much trouble in the world   Think about your troubles   We spell trouble   Trouble in the city, trouble in the farm   Trouble, trouble, trouble   Nothin' but trouble   Oh trouble set me free   I think I'm in trouble   Trouble come running   Trouble where the kids are   You end up here in trouble and strife   I won't be trouble no more   The trouble boys came in   To get my baby back from the trouble boys   What's the trouble down here?   Knowin' the trouble down here below   He was having trouble   That's the trouble in this world   Oh Lord I'm sorry, but there's trouble on the line   Does it become you troublemaker   'Cause trouble man don't get in my way   You ain't gonna trouble poor me anymore   Well I pulled on trouble's braids   But remember troubles don't always last   Nobody knows my trouble   Bad luck and trouble   I'm through with all my trouble   Now I'm blue and the trouble with me is you   When a woman gets in trouble everybody throws her down   There ain't but one thing worth my trouble in mind   Wrap your troubles in dreams   You've got your troubles and I've got mine

4

I knew you were trouble when you walked in   One kiss and that spells trouble   Trouble, trouble, trouble, trouble, trouble   Looking for some trouble tonight   Never woulda seen the trouble that I'm in   Trouble's what feels good to me   Papa don't preach, I'm in trouble deep   She's trouble, in a word get closer to the fire   Trouble seemed so far away   I dance to escape my troubles   I'm not looking for trouble   We in trouble but you won't meet me at the bridge   We don't cause trouble, we just ride

XXII: Trouble on the Line[36]

Poem XXI[37] of *Spring and All* concludes "so lascivious / and still" and segues into XXII,[38] "so much depends / upon" (Williams 74) — the rest is on every schoolchild's mind, or used to be, perhaps. People who don't think they've memorized a line of verse can say most or all of William Carlos Williams's "The Red Wheel Barrow," only it isn't called that, and the only "the" in the poem indicates some (white) chickens.

This may sound finicky or even ingenuous, but here's the trouble: We don't know what we know. We have the words but forget the form that keeps them coming back to us. Worse, we don't have the context. XXII is not a stand-alone poem, it's a proof. It's in conversation with the "poem"[39] before it, but also with the "prose"[40] that follows.

Let's see this Trouble Song in prose stanzas, rather than graphs.

And how about a word from our sponsor?

> The fixed categories into which life is divided must always hold. These things are normal — essential to every activity. But they exist — but not as dead dissections. (Williams 75)

---

36 Thanks to participants in the New School Graduate Writing Program seminar DEEP SURFACE (fall 2013), where some of these readings took shape.
37 Or is it Chapter XXI, or just XXI?
38 Do we dare call it enjambment? No.
39 Let's be careful here in anticipation of what follows XXII.
40 Is prose poetry in sentences? Yes, prose poetry is in sentences. As for prose, let's say prose is poetry that doesn't know how it sounds, unless it's prose poetry, which too often still doesn't know how it sounds, distracted as it is by its lack of line breaks. All writing knows how it looks, but some poems look like prose.

From here Williams proceeds (as he has preceded) to show us what he has done,[41] and what he wants to do. *Spring and All*[42] is like that, a manifesto in action. Whereas Charles Bernstein in "Artifice of Absorption"[43] show&tells us what he has been doing since at least 1976's *The Veil*, while proceeding with a poetics that is surface and depth, Williams sets a program for what his poems will be by the time he finishes the present collection. He describes his poetics into existence, nearly abolishing the distinction between poetry and prose while insisting on that distinction:

> [T]here is no use denying that prose and poetry are not by any means the same IN INTENTION. But what then is prose? There is no need for it to approach poetry except to be weakened. (77–78)

But then: "Is what I have written prose ? The only answer is that form in prose ends with the end of that which is being communicated" (78). And here let us pause to admire that isolated question mark. Is it a typesetter's error? No, it must be real! Or must anyway be real, even intentional!

Is Williams's prose approaching poetry? Aspiring to it, even? And these are different aims: The first is an address, a correspondence; the second is perhaps what Williams describes as ends with the end. Let's put a fine point on it: Poem XXII becomes itself, XXII, because it breaks the barriers of form while

---

41 and call out our bad education, which will proceed to cast XXII as an isolated riddle; the trouble with us is we can't see and read at the same time

42 Better named in previous editions (though New Directions' 2011 standalone volume is commendable in numerous ways, including C.D. Wright's feeling-it intro — method if not methodical, and better for that) by a ligature (perhaps courtesy of an expedient typesetter): *Spring & All*.

43 Bernstein notes that he completed his essay in verse in 1986; it formed the front-and-centerpiece of his essay collection *A Poetics* (1992); dates become important later this sentence.

making form matter (again and henceforth). The prose that follows is free to see itself as poetry: as form and sense.[44]

We remember the prose, in prosaic line breaks:

So much depends upon
A red wheel barrow
Glazed with rainwater
Beside the white chickens

How different this is from "so much depends / upon // a red wheel / barrow // glazed with rain / water // beside the white / chickens"! Three stanzas we love for their koan-like demeanor, their question as (unpunctuated) statement. Just what is it that depends upon what, again?

What we have here is a structure that makes sense: 4 stanzas of 2 lines each, always 3 words followed by 1, with the following nearly palindromic syllabic scheme: 4/2 // 3/2 // 3/2 // 4/2.[45] More to love: the modernist insistence on the level playing field of lower case.

Those partner lines to each couplet are the most consistent formal element of the poem. Always 2 syllables, always a revelation without being a surprise. They always dangle and usually hinge. The first ("upon") is the most formally obvious but also the most catchy. Even if we don't remember the line breaks, Williams taught many of us how to break lines between the first and second stanza of this poem. Revelation, though, (be)comes cheap after a while. Prepositions make for obvious line breaks, particularly when they get visual (as in the tired "over /" and "/ under" break). But this one has more than the sweetness of

---

[44] Poetry, then, is not only prose that hears itself; it is prose that sees itself and shows what it says.
[45] If we think of this in terms of blues annotation (or a schematic version of blues scholarship), we have an ABBA structure, which is more properly palindromic.

first blush. The stanza break is excruciating[46] if you look too closely at it. Our dangling prep hangs over a cliff—depends upon what? — then gives us this marvelous red wheel

barrow

.

Compare Williams's meticulous but somehow naturalistic breaks to the prosaic parsing we recall. One poem is memorable (and memorizable), and the other is bland as fuck. A forgetful 1. So we remember something we can no longer take seriously, while remembering it wrong, but only remembering it because of the formal precision of the original, which we cannot see.

Once we look at the form, and consider it in context ("The fixed categories into which life is divided must always hold" takes on the force of dramatic imperative rather than description; our hinges keep us whole), the structure speaks to us. The koan becomes an illustration.

XXII is not an imagist poem. Nor does it present an image, but the image of an image. 1 thing becomes 4, but it also becomes words, and a poem.

If we insist on investigating the image, we find 3 things[47] right away:

wheel barrow
rain water
chickens.

---

46 because unbearably exquisite, like a hair so fine it pierces your eye
47 & 23 years later, *Paterson* will insist "no ideas but in things." Let's play the numbers game: S&A first arrives in '23, *Paterson* 23 years after that. XXII has 22 syllables, and its middle 2 stanzas go 3/2, 3/2, which is backwards & slashed for 23 23.

1 thing becomes 4 formally, but maybe imagistically, 3 things become 4. But our 3-count only counts the last 3 stanzas, cuz that's where we see things clearly. Stanza 1 is all *so much* and *depends on,* so we don't see ourselves seeing through language, or thinking we do. The 4th thing[48] is language. We see it in the form, as form.

What depends on what? Does the wheel barrow/rain water/chicken need language, or vice versa?

As the language goes on to say,[49] "There is no confusion — only difficulties" (78).

---

48 found much later, in the 1st stanza
49 Recall Rosmarie Waldrop, who repeats in "Alarms & Excursions," "language thinks for us" (46), which we misread as *language speaks for us*. On the next page, she elaborates her initial proposition: "So, while language thinks for us, there is no guarantee that it will be in the direction we like." Let's just say language speaks us, and call it a day.

One Kind Favor ("See That My Grave Is Kept Clean")

On behalf of the dead, the living are nostalgic for life. The dead bear this patronage as they must: They sing on. The song does not change when the singer leaves the world, though we hear a strain previously hidden to us. Perhaps the singer pre-empts our concerns[50] with instructions, but they twist in the passage. *Bury my body by the side of the road* formerly implied *You treat me so mean*. Now it signs off, *What do I care?*[51]

†††

Blind Lemon Jefferson has a last request, *one kind favor* he'll ask you[52] over and over until the recording passes completely into the aural fog that already obscures his appeal.[53] We can't imagine the man alive, singing the song, paying forward the trib-

---

50 or our agenda: If the dead keep singing, they sing for us as much as they sing to us
51 In Robert Johnson's version of this floating lyric, he grants permission — *You may bury my body down by the highway side* — then translates the line sotto voce, *Baby I don't care where you bury my body when I'm dead and gone*. But he's already made the accusation, also from the side of his mouth, *You know you ain't doing me right*. We believe everything this man says, after his claim that he walked with the devil. He sells it with the (unhidden) strain in his voice when he sings *Me and the Devil*. That *me* is every bit as terrifying and unspeakable as *I'm gonna beat my woman until I get satisfied*.[a] It's certainly leagues scarier than *the Devil* (which is not comforting company). Here's a man beyond kindness, and here's the song for which he traded his soul: "Me and the Devil Blues."
   a So unspeakable, for Gil Scott-Heron, that in his version of the song, he sings the line *I'm gonna see my woman until I get satisfied*.
52 Much later, Bob Dylan will ask one kind favor, that you allow him just one more chance, but Jefferson knows he's already had his last chance.
53 though it does nothing to disperse its affect; on the contrary, it binds us, or hides us together

ute he demands[54] — and it is a demand, polite as it sounds.[55] It also comes across plaintive, so we shroud him in longing for the breath he expels in the song. But the request itself, *see that my grave is kept clean*, resists our sentimentality[56] even as it appears to beg it. The clean grave is no tribute to life, and the dead have no use for flowers or songs. The one kind favor is asked of you, but you disappear in the request itself — just as the task is never completed. You become witness without a body, or you pay forward[57] when you too pass into the fog.

†††

Lou Reed stretches Jefferson's two-minute-forty-two-second plea into seven-and-a-half minutes of recording static transmuted into guitar feedback, texture and sustain. He knows the singer is dead, even if he's thinking of Jefferson.[58] He also knows he too will pay forward[59] the request. Meanwhile, Jefferson sings on, blind as he may be to the world without end.

---

54 or putting a down payment on it; the song, however, is free, as is the use of the lines he takes (and gives), so though he expects a return, he can't receive it, and gives away his song, even if it isn't his to give

55 *One kind favor I ask of you* suggests "if it isn't too much trouble," but as we will see and hear, it might just be trouble enough.

56 "No trouble," we reply.

57 or hand off (trouble or no trouble), though you don't benefit from the gift; perhaps you pay backward, though Jefferson can hardly benefit, except as legend in our minds — and who benefits from that?

58 The song was recorded live for *The Harry Smith Project: Anthology of American Folk Music Revisited*. Songs from Smith's anthology were recorded by multiple artists during three concerts in 1999 and 2001, then released in 2006 as a four-CD box set. If you search today for Reed's version, it will undoubtedly carry a new date — October 27, 2013, the day Reed passed into the fog of the song.

59 Here, then, is where the kind favor is advanced. The singer passes his request (if it isn't too much trouble) to the next singer (and listener), keeping the grave (and others in turn) clean, keeping the song (also a grave, or at least a headstone) in the world, wherever that is.

Down the Line

> — *John, I // sd, which was not his / name,*
> *the darkness sur- / rounds us...*
> — Robert Creeley, "I Know a Man"

If, as has been suggested, trouble has a cousin — problem — the two might be confused for one another. The singer — the trouble singer — knows better, but isn't telling the truth she knows. Problems have solutions, at least 'pataphysical ones;[60] trouble is insoluble, even in/with whiskey. José González (as trouble singer, if not speaker) sees problems down the line, and knows he's right.[61] We hear trouble in the echo from "Trouble on the Line,"[62] and we hear it in his voice, even as he promises problems.[63]

A clue, then, to the difference between problem and [trouble][64] (or problem as trouble, or vice versa): A problem has

---

60 Of course, 'pataphysics describes imaginary solutions to *imaginary* problems. (Thanks to Talan Memmott for the distinction.) And Trouble Songs are in our heads, if not only in our heads (like trouble itself, whatever it may be).

61 The couplet that opens "Down the Line" is a variation on the AAB blues form, where *I know that I'm right* takes the place of A-line repetition, simultaneously providing the B-line.[a] Such re-placement is exactly the problem here. Repetitions (with slight differences) of the coming *same mistake twice* refrain will underscore the blues-form adaptation.

   a   If we hear the line this way. If we believe the lyric sheet rather than our ears, the line is *I know they're not mine*. It's a better line, if perhaps less formally suggestive in a musicological sense (cf. the blues connection). On the one hand a hard rhyme (line/mine) replaces a more intriguing and less stable off rhyme (line/right). However, the lyric sheet version intensifies interpersonal tension, and positions the singer more explicitly as harbinger. The insistence of *I'm right* suggests disharmony and doubt, but *they're not mine* is an ominous twist, even a threat. Close listening has the line both ways in the song, and the ambiguity is an improvement on either line.

62 and as reverb in the telephone game of floating versions (on March 8, 2014, an *All Music Guide* search retrieves 913,215 results for "trouble on the line"; by the time the echo drops "trouble," results are 1,316,216)

63 Promises, promises...

64 that is, hidden trouble

a solution, but *problems* presents a series — potentially a whole lot of trouble.[65] So "Down the Line" hides trouble: first in its title, then in the song — absence, then replacement. But the refrain that swallows the song — *Don't let the darkness eat you up* — is all portent and no pretending.[66] It's also, after many listens, a cumulative[67] warning — not an affirmation, as at first it might have seemed.[68] The darkness is coming, the darkness has come, the darkness is here.

And here we are, in trouble again.

---

65 We — including the singer — may have troubles, but we don't need them to have worry. Trouble is trouble enough.

66 The opening couplet, then, might be an attempt to avoid the AAB refrain (and the problems the couplet foretells) — where the repeated first blues line, which often sets up a problem as a series (or same problem, different day) that is repeated (or repeatedly foils the singer), would be the *same mistake twice*.[a] The attempt seems to fail in several ways. We might hear that *same mistake* as the false assurance of the second line — in either variation, though it is particularly poignant on the lyric sheet. Either the first two lines are the same mistake twice (reiterated as *I know I'm right*) or the second line reads the first incorrectly (where *they're not mine* fails to recognize problems as one's own, and the sage is a fool). By song's end, the problems of repetition (particularly if repetition — AAB — was to be avoided) worsen in accumulation, as the song is reduced to one line repeated over and over: *Don't let the darkness eat you up.* Who then is the you in that line?

a As the second song on *In Our Nature*, "Down the Line" might itself be the same mistake twice, and it might be a (failed) corrective to the first song, which also flirts with the repetition-compulsion death drive of the AAB blues form. *How long, / How long are you willing to go* suggests the AA form, and subsequent lines deliver a poetics of the B line (with a nod in the mirror to AA repetition): *Punch line after punch line leaving us sore, leaving us sore.* Here the B line substitutes the blues' self-deprecatory comic relief with word play as suffering as eternal recurrence.

67 and cumulus, as gathering and compiling clouds-becoming-darkness

68 Thanks to Claire Donato for sharing this observation.

Trouble in Heart

The trouble with a broken heart is it never stops bleeding. Angel Olsen sings either about trouble's end or mend[69] in "Unfucktheworld." Either way, she[70] lets trouble into her heart on song one of her 2014 album.[71] It's a risk and a wager in a world brimming with love songs and trouble. But if the heart has more than endless trouble — if the troubled heart won't mend — we have something more than heartache. We have a wound that will not heal. And even if it did, we'd never see the scar among all that blood. And how would the wound ever congeal? Perhaps the troubled heart is already broken, already bleeding, already beating its regular irregular beat. Perhaps the heart is always already in trouble, always awash in its own blood, always dubbing itself one more version of the beat.

Let's refrain with a difference: The trouble with a broken heart is it never stops bleeding, and how would we know if it did?

---

69 Accounts differ, but this ear hears *mend,* which has the advantage of mixing up the rhyme scheme, so *end* in the first line of the second verse (which sounds like a chorus but isn't repeated) doesn't rhyme with itself in the third line.
70 the singer, if not Olsen
71 *Burn Your Fire for No Witness,* an album of heartache released three days after V Day

The Circle

> *Can the circle be unbroken?*
> — The Carter Family et al.

> *You're caught in a vicious circle / Surrounded by your so-called friends*
> — Lou Reed, "Vicious Circle"

Say a community surrounds us. Depending on where we stand within that community, this is to be desired, we are told.[72] And if we're in a community long enough, we may know what it's like to be contained there. The tighter the circle, the less likely one can get in.[73] If life itself is a circle, it's broken and unbroken in each lifetime, as birth and death are the prerequisites for every life.[74] Or: The broken circle may not be unbroken, except by the record's turn.

Perhaps that home in the sky of which they sing is no comfort to us, either because it won't be enough like the earthly home we sometimes love, or it sounds too much like the one we thought to escape. Or we reject such promise as too unlikely in any case, or we're ready at the bell to truly and forever call it a day. Or again to return to previous tropes, the record will play after we're gone, and that's just fine.

†††

---

72 often by the community

73 or out

74 Death and taxes are at best two-thirds of our obligations: *It's such a gamble when you get a face,* as Richard Hell has it in "Blank Generation," eager as he is to roll the dice (*I was saying let me out of here before I was even born,* he delivers himself before the hand is dealt). *Tell me why is the pain of birth / Lighter borne than the pain of death?* argues Joanna Newsom on her song "Divers." We are born against this plashing. *There's only three things for sure: taxes, death and trouble,* sings Marvin Gaye in "Trouble Man." Taxes and death catch up to us, but we're born into trouble.

There's a dark and a troubled side of life, The Carter Family sings before insisting we keep on the sunny side, *keep on the sunny side of life.*[75] But the storm returns to crush our hopes,[76] but the sun will return, *keep on the sunny side of life.* The third verse, where we pray and hope, fails to deliver us from the promise of that first line,[77] nor does verse three regain the irresolvable, dialectical beauty of those first two verses.

†††

Should the flood come, The Staple Singers remind us (in "Wade in the Water") not just that we cannot walk on it, or that we may be born again (baptized by blood or water, dressed in red or white), but that to trouble the water is to get in.[78] Their "Will[79] the Circle Be Unbroken" adds a blue note to the song's final accord.

†††

The trouble singer is beyond the grave,[80] which the recording[81] both allows and attests. Once we discover the recording that outlasts the singer, we suspect the recording[82] is always already an afterlife. The singer has a foot in the grave,[83] so to speak. This

---

75 "Keep on the Sunny Side"
76 Of course, we saw it coming, as the opening lines of "Can the Circle Be Unbroken" attest:
    I was standing / By the window / On one cold and cloudy day
77 As, elsewhere in another time, Morrissey will begin his album *Vauxhall and I* (1994) with a promise he may or may not keep: *There's gonna be some trouble.*
78 though the agency, if not the refrain, is God's: *God's gonna trouble the water*
79 Which sounds more inevitable, if not more possible, than "Can the Circle Be Unbroken?"
80 if not in that home in the sky
81 if not the performance
82 and the performance
83 and the afterworld

allows[84] an irrational[85] belief that the singer can report from the afterlife.[86]

"Curse my name when I'm gone" is the trouble singer's calling card.[87] If and when the singer leaves town after her song,[88] she symbolically enacts a final departure; abandoning her immediate authority (as mic controller[89] and presence presenting the song) also amplifies the power of the song as witness from beyond. She unbreaks and breaks the circle, singing the way in and the way out of community.

Of course, to the extent the Trouble Song does its trick[90] and convinces the audience its troubles are both evoked and put at bay, the trouble singer is imperiled by the end of the spell. In particular, she's in danger of being hung with a sign that says troublemaker.[91] As a parting gift, the singer takes the blame for whatever troubles she leaves behind, but she has to leave to make that possible.[92]

---

84 and promotes
85 or non-rational, but no less transporting
86 thus achieving an impossible critical position from which one might see the world from a remove, which is of course frustrated by the fact that the singer or recording appears in the world
87 or payment for her ticket out of town
88 often an exceedingly good idea (with or without mic drop), as will be suggested soon
89 figurative in a remote historical context; see Appendix C for the Electronic Literature Organization 2014 conference panel presentation "Troubadours & Troublemakers," which introduces a contemporary trouble singer figure, the DJ (who may be accompanied by an MC and/or a Mixmaster)
90 magic, we insist
91 again, see Appendix C, and consider the often overlooked (or even indistinct) difference between talking about something and making it happen
92 and to avoid the direct consequences of blame, which extend to pillory; leaving, she wagers (and leverages) renown

The song itself can't fix people's troubles,[93] though it might allow singer/listeners to reflect on their troubles[94] in a way that benefits the community.[95] At least (and maybe at most), the song offers respite in a communal environment, but that's not a simple or simply escapist pleasure.[96] We pursue a particular role for the trouble singer,[97] and it's tied to the duration of the song as much as the material of the song. Let the record complicate this.

---

[93] Only problems have solutions, as attested in the second episode of the *Breaking Bad* spinoff *Better Call Saul*, in which the kingpin Tuco Salamanca reappears (or pre-appears) to invoke the difference between trouble and problem (and dispel the former by reducing it to the latter, then erasing it): "They say I'm in trouble," his suburban desert grandmother tells him; "There's no problem," he assures her.

[94] and their commonality

[95] but maybe let's not blame the trouble singer for this, either

[96] or gift, or curse (the spell might work, but the hangover might be brutal, with all apologies to and for the *Buffy the Vampire Slayer* storyline in which, having attained her black robe in witchcraft, Willow Rosenberg does magic like Ozzy Osbourne does drugs)

[97] as observed in Trouble Songs

I'm a Fool to Want You

Is Bob Dylan's *Shadows in the Night* (2015) a slanted, elliptical album cover of Frank Sinatra's *Where Are You?* (1957)? The question looks so closely at the track list — four of 10 songs on Dylan's album appear on its ostensible wellspring[98] — that it fails to hear the songs. The interview Dylan gave to Robert Love at *The Independent* (published February 7, 2015) positions Dylan in relation to both the Great American Songbook he seemed long ago to burn,[99] and to Sinatra as interpreter of the classics.[100] Of course, Frank's voice is at a different stage of his career in '57 than Dylan's is in '15, even if Dylan's latter-day crooning on this record makes a convincing case that he's smoother than ever.[101]

---

98 and all 10 were recorded there or elsewhere by Sinatra

99 Dylan's eponymous first album (1962) is heavy on traditional songs and blues covers (or appropriations, if you prefer), and concludes with Blind Lemon Jefferson's plea, "See That My Grave Is Kept Clean," whereas his sophomore effort the following year turns decisively to original material (with the exception of the traditional "Corrina, Corrina," which he baldly steals in his (re-)definitive rendition, and "Honey, Just Allow Me One More Chance," for which his version takes a co-credit).[a] However, his underrated (in their time) early '90s all-cover albums (*Good as I Been to You* and *World Gone Wrong*) served notice that Dylan hadn't burned any bridges in song.

    a A few years later, in 1969, Dylan would borrow Roebuck "Pops" Staples's voice on *Nashville Skyline* — how else to account for his astonishing (and temporary) vocal transformation? — which was otherwise free of covers.

100 The interview presents Dylan the musicologist and dry-as-ice comedian, thrilled to be drilled on matters pertaining to his trade. After a lengthy round of questioning, Love thanks Dylan for his generous responses. Dylan: "The last time I did an interview, the guy wanted to know about everything except the music. Man, I'm just a musician, you know? People have been doing that to me since the Sixties — they ask questions like they would ask a medical doctor or a psychiatrist or a professor or a politician. Why? Why are you asking me these things?"

101 or that nice pipes were never his thing and who ever went to him for easy listening? These songs will kill you if you sing them straight, or the ghost of Frank will fuck you up.

But *Shadows in the Night* opens with a clue that Dylan has another reference[102] in mind.[103] While *Where Are You?* begins with the eponymous track, Dylan heads straight for the middle of Frank's set,[104] "I'm a Fool to Want You."[105] This is the same place Billie Holiday begins her penultimate album, *Lady in Satin* (1958).[106] At this late date, Lady Day's voice is a different instrument than it was in the '30s and '40s, but it is an instrument she knows well. Far from betraying her, Holiday's voice is in her command — or rather, she knows how to listen to its demands. *Shadows* shows just how well Dylan has absorbed her lesson.

---

102 and other trouble
103 and let's pause here to note trouble's passage through the end of the end of the album, among the final lines of "That Lucky Old Sun": *Show me that river / Take me across / and wash all my troubles away*. Perhaps the bridge has been burned, or "troubles" cover the "bridge," or Dylan is singing to the bridge, begging it take him to the other side.
104 the two sets double-knotted by a lyric from "What'll I Do": *With just a photograph to tell my troubles to*
105 We would have loved to hear that Dylan opened his Vegas show the day he won the Nobel Prize — how beautiful it is that he debuted his laurel crown in Vegas — with this song, but happily settle for his closer, "Why Try to Change Me Now" (which appears on *Shadows in the Night* and on Sinatra's *No One Cares*). The writing is on the wall. In any case, Dylan's trouble shield was up as he refused committee calls.
106 Holiday's set has this one song in common with *Where Are You?* but also includes three songs that appear on Sinatra's epic sad-bastard companion, *In the Wee Small Hours* (1955): "I Get Along Without You Very Well," "Glad to Be Unhappy," and "I'll Be Around." In his *AllMusic* overview of *Where Are You?*, Stephen Thomas Erlewine further complicates the relationship by noting the influence of Holiday's ballads on the album's tempos.

Lay It Down

> *The contract was that each would give what they had; that each would try, the singer speaking as he or she sang, the song speaking as it was sung, the listener speaking as he or she listened, to mean what they said.*
> — Greil Marcus

We hear it wrong: *The History of America in Ten Songs*.[107] In Greil Marcus's voice, the elusively simple, droll, rote, compulsive top-10 format[108] hyperarticulates into a survey of every song — or many of the songs — that cross(es) his mind as he mentions one song, calling every version, every listening occasion, or some of them, most of them, all. And all the ways we'll hear them one day, give or take a few, as we forget yesterday tomorrow, a concentrated effort that absorbs and absolves itself. We remember everything, of course.[109] So the song is unbearable, too much and never enough.[110]

Throughout Marcus's oeuvre of music (as culture) writing, the thing is to find the song — whether it's a band on stage or in studio working its way into a cover or trying to make one of its own songs sing, or it's a teenager in her room expanding the world wearing deeper grooves into a record that finally found

---

107 The cover says *The History of Rock 'n' Roll in Ten Songs*.
108 distended echo — dub version — of his long-running column, *Real Life Rock Top Ten*
109 Happily, we remember also to forget. The Trouble Song is that reminder.
110 In the early days of MTV, when the network promised all the ill-conceived videos you could stand, '80s pop icons like David Bowie, Cyndi Lauper, Billy Idol, Boy George and The Police appeared in spots concluding with the slogan "Too much is never enough." L.A. alternative rock radio station KROQ (if this memory is to be trusted) spliced together and appropriated a choral version of the slogan: *Too much... yeah, too much... is never... is never... is never... is never... enough.*

her.[111] Marcus finds people finding the song.[112] And losing it to find it again.[113]

Meanwhile, the song has no idea where we are, and barely cares.

It calls us anyway.

And yes, trouble finds us, sings us, singing it.

Listen to the first elongated[114] guitar break on The Feelies' *The Good Earth*. It's the color of the cover photo, Autumn. The singer will come back eventually, but you'll hardly hear him. Here we're in the woods with guitars as far as the eye can see. The song fades just like it came in, but less loud. Then not there at all.

Soon enough, something will take its place. And if we're very lucky, it will come back the way it left, only in reverse.

Every song plays itself, or it stops, for however many seasons, being a song.

A number of seasons pass, verses on the radio between commercial breaks and talk.

We exit the woods, enter a clearing, pass through another wood.

---

[111] As Marcus reads Thora Burch as Enid Coleslaw in *Ghost World*, listening over and over to Skip James's "Devil Got My Woman," convinced, per Marcus, the song was made for her alone — how rare then that we get to watch her listen.

[112] Or, perhaps and also, being found by the song which sought them all along, Amy Winehouse giving us the song that waited 48 years for her: in Marcus's telling, "To Know Him Is to Love Him."

[113] As does Steve Buscemi's sad sack record collector Seymour, who assures Coleslaw there are no other records like "Devil Got My Woman." He might as well leave out the word "other."

[114] or discursive, in the sense that it spans subjects as well as time

Castle Leferbvre has ceased to enjoy itself.[115] The long gap between the bottom of hills catches up. The room, anchored by speakers. Sink running. Fan for a time still on. Maybe what they sang about is true. Maybe present.[116]

Now that the old spot came back. Barking at the door.[117] A shadow in the light.

†††

"[E]verything comes back harder, scarier, in a split second at the end, as if the fine story of sex and whiskey Johnson has told was a con, softening up the listener for a truth the singer can tell only by concealing it" (Marcus 152). Robert Johnson, back to the audience, telling you everything but his troubles — in a sleight of hand that offers nothing but trouble —, selling instead his devil con, the magic of which is (he'll have) you telling it down the line. So you carry troubles that are not your own, until they are. Johnson kept the devil away with a song, and still the song plays, as he bet it would — but the devil caught him anyway, the extra sting his whiskey served.

We always serve the song until it serves our final order. Lay down now, once more.

---

115 Henri Lefebvre's *Toward an Architecture of Enjoyment*, written in 1973 and discovered years later among his papers, appearing in English translation in 2014, describes the castle as a frustrated pleasure palace. The will to power founders on its own insatiable desire to conquer, a drama the private lord of any record collection plays out in modest digs, as above.
116 A foundational argument of Marcus's book is that the truly singular song casts away linear time, spinning in a perpetual now that remains up to date — perhaps in part because it both pre-dates and post-dates the song, availing itself of the lessons that follow it. ("Song" and "now" here become exchangeable.) And here the cover leans its shadow over our spines.
117 A man barking on his knees, as Robert Johnson is said to have met the next world.

Cause You're Mine

When Nina Simone sings *[I] put a spell on you*,[118] it's not a song anymore.[119]

(Screamin' Jay Hawkins's spirited 1956 version[120] is made to disappear.)

It's a curse that sends the singer to hell.

Simone's single, and its eponymous album, *I Put a Spell On You*,[121] are released[122] in 1965[123] (four years after her version of "Trouble in Mind"). The word trouble need not be intoned in the song — if it were, this would not be a Trouble Song.[124] There is no gesture to spare the listener from actual trouble: the scapegoats are slaughtered, the albatross comes home to ro(o)(a)(s)t.

The singer/listener in full affect: Simone is entranced. *You're mine. Your mine. Your mind.*[125]

---

118 the I barely there — breath trailing to the afterworld — or not yet there, and in any case gone
119 though it's also a song, as "trouble" is exchanged for trouble (or, here, vice versa)
120 A cover of his own song from 1949, remade under the influence of Italian Swiss Colony Muscatel courtesy of a label head trying to make something happen. Nick Tosches, in *Unsung Heroes of Rock 'n' Roll*, tells the story of Hawkins coming to and reckoning with the debauched track after the record's release 10 days later. "All those drunken screams and groans and yells ... my God," Hawkins recalls what Tosches describes as "the monster that haunted him ever after" (159–160).
121 *I PUT / A SPELL / ON YOU* per the Philips cover graphic.
122 not released, unleashed — but not set free
123 transposing the digits — presto! — on its predecessor
124 or it would not be a "Trouble" Song — read on
125 The speaker is not always the singer, but Simone asserts *"I Put a Spell on You" is mine*. She sings to the song as the song sings to her.

As gender trouble, the performative magic of Simone's version is to take a song that might have spoken to[126] her, and speak through it.[127]

Her delivery reveals a darkness[128] concealed in Hawkins's camp: The singer is under the spell of the song.[129]

Where the beloved rejects her heart, so she offers[130] her soul.

Opening strings rope everyone in. Piano palpitates hearts. Vocals kill us all.

The second *spell* is a grave.[131] The hearse-chasing saxophone is a miserable taunt, an inadequate complaint. The third *spell* is a false apology that dares you to believe it. The song ends too soon, no relief.

No trouble, nor "trouble," the singer is not there. Only the record, a recording absence, recorded absence, spinning a spell, spinning in a spell. That which is absent, as absence. Your mine.

---

126 or at
127 And here's the trouble with singing: whether the singer sings the song or the song sings the singer. Trouble trumps both, singing singer and song.
128 Ta-Nehisi Coates writes, in "Nina Simone's Face": "That voice, inevitably, calls us to look at Nina Simone's face, and for a brief moment, understand that the hate we felt, that the mockery we dispensed, was unnatural, was the fruit of conjurations and the shadow of plunder. We look at Nina Simone's face and the lie is exposed and we are shamed. ... We look at Nina Simone's face and a terrible truth comes into view — there was nothing wrong with her. But there is something deeply wrong with us." His *we* is distinct from his *us*, though they are integral, warped by racist projection and absorption. Simone appears in the song, sings to us, and we are captivated.
129 Once we recognize the auto-curse, we may better understand Hawkins's astonishment on hearing his 1956 recording.
130 surrenders, as one lets go of what one holds dear, for what one holds dear
131 *Be-cause you're mine,* and here the beheaded *cause* in the opening line has a precisely enunciated prefix that arrives as accusation.

Part Four

BACK IN TROUBLE

You see, ah, trouble down the tracks?
— Thomas Pynchon, *Bleeding Edge*

the year in which this particular round / of troubles began
— C.D. Wright, *One With Others*

The song is a séance in which the living and the dead change places until everyone is dead.
— Greil Marcus, "Disappearance and Forgetting"

Return to Trouble, That Lonesome Town

> *But "a poetry collection is like a record collection." (R. Maurer)*
> — Donato Mancini

There's a moment in *Six Feet Under*, after Ruth's new husband George has refurbished a bomb shelter he discovers on the mortuary property. Ruth finds him there, sitting on the bed, looking up (for once) at her. She asks him what he's doing in there and he says *I live here now*.[1] I'd look for the scene to check my memory and add detail, but I don't have to. Can't. I live *here* now.

In Trouble. Here in song.

Since I began writing *Trouble Songs* in earnest a few years ago now (nearly seven, at this moment, the day after the day after David Bowie joined the singers who exist in this world as song), this is where I live. I finished Part 3 and told myself and others that *Trouble Songs* was done.[2] But I never left the lonesome town of Trouble — the town where we are alone together, perhaps happily so, where we share "trouble" if not our troubles.

I no longer look for trouble, but it still finds me. And when it sings to me, when a word stands out in a song I've heard a hundred times, I hear it with a queer nostalgia — with what I might call kitsch, as I once tried to define it: nostalgia for something you didn't experience. Perhaps that's a definition of the sublime, or at least the devil's advocacy for the sublime. But I wonder in those moments a light is cast on a lyric I might have known so well: Have I written through a subconscious awareness of this lyric? How long have I heard Trouble Songs, or how long had I heard them before I knew what to call them? If "trouble" wasn't a word I notice in song, a word that opens a lower door, that

---

[1] He practically sings it, so let's leave off the quotes and italicize as we have done with sung text.

[2] always or often with the asterisk that I might write another part some day

rattles bones, that drops a shadow over the anatomical heart or places a black felt cutout heart over it, if I didn't hear dark wings flapping in those two syllables, I would never have ended up in Trouble.

I am where I do not want to leave. Which is maybe a way of thinking about the world, like it or not.

So how do you come back to Trouble when you never left? And how do you go on?

I don't mean that last sentence as a plea to the devil or the muse.[3] I wouldn't be here if I didn't know where I might be headed.[4]

What happened is Part 3 ended and the road of Part 4 was unclear(ed) or indiscernible. I hadn't even found the wood. But in the meanwhile, as I imagined maybe it was done, for now or forever: I kept hearing "trouble," not so much as something I'd taken with me as something that took me with it.

So there's *maybe I should have written about that,* and there's *why didn't I hear that "trouble" before,* and there's the purgatory of the end without an end to trouble. The forest without the trees.

And there's *I live here now.*

So here's what I propose: Go down with me into the songs that find us. For what appears to me as well appears to you, as Whitman, that conflicted character, once sort of said. He too is the ghost — and the demon[5] — of America. Robert Johnson also walked with the devil, then sang songs of himself that draw us

---

3   nor to the devil muse
4   down, down, down, a katabasic chorus of the soon-enough dead
5   Ask poet CAConrad, who's made a compelling case for Whitman the racist poster boy for (or voice and witness to) America's troubled foundation. See "From Whitman to Walmart" online at *Harriet*, poetryfoundation.org/harriet/2015/06/from-whitman-to-walmart.

in, whether or not we can repeat after him: *I'm gonna beat my woman / Until I get satisfied.*[6]

There's nothing to catch up with, just as there's no place to run when the body is where the self, however it is constructed, resides. We live here now.

And sure, *here* is a record room, an echoing hall that is also a bomb shelter, in and out of the world, contingent. We escape to ourselves, never from ourselves.

So as "trouble" finds me, I'll write these Trouble Songs.[7] As I will and as I won't—which is to say I won't make a corn-whiskey-filled prison[8] of *Trouble Songs*. But this might open a few more doors—in the floor, the ceiling, or one of the walls. C'mon in.

---

[6] Gil Scott-Heron's evasion—*I'm gonna see my woman*—on his "Me and the Devil Blues" adaptation for his last album, *I'm New Here*, tries to provide an exit, or access to the genius adjacent the horror of another time (and another exchange of oppression). If we're lucky, we'll horrify the future in turn, with our own meanness, or own blind eyes, our own willingness to go there.

[7] Difficult usage, here: If Trouble Song refers to an individual song that fits this classification, and *Trouble Songs* refers to these collected writings about Trouble Songs, and individual chapters may also be seen as Trouble Songs, how do we treat this term when it refers to a selection of Trouble Songs but not the whole collection? And how's there a whole when the whole is growing?

[8] Datestamp: as I wrote this sentence, I noticed Bowie's breathsound on the opening musical section of ★'s second track, "'Tis a Pity She Was a Whore." I'd noticed it before, when he was still breathing, but now I hear it differently, as the recorded breath, the promise that its counterpart will quiet.[a] Now also the titular gallows humor is apparent, and Bowie is himself the erstwhile whore: *'Tis my fate I suppose.*

    [a] and/or "the phantasm that the mechanical reproduction of the silenced voice emits," as Fred Moten conjures it (*In the Break* 118)

Death's Head, Proud Flesh[9]

Death shadows text and trouble emerges, even as it recedes; or the dead recede from trouble, leave it behind for the ones who can't do without it.

January takes another light. Just as David Bowie's last two videos, for "★"[10] and "Lazarus," foreshadow the obvious[11] only after Bowie's passing, a poet who departed with even greater haste left the sleepless remainder with death-charged books.

The American poet C.D. Wright, in *Cooling Time: An American Poetry Vigil*, in a passage from the previous decade that made the rounds of the living in the wake of January 13, 2016 feeds, writing her headstone, anticipating ours: *Poetry is the language of intensity. Because we are all going to die, an expression of intensity is justified* (61).[12]

Like Bowie, Wright left us with new work, though her book of poetry *ShallCross* was forthcoming at her sudden passing,[13] so

---

9 for Danniel Schoonebeek and Claire Donato
10 The song includes a choral provocation — *Somebody else took his place and bravely cried: / I'm a blackstar* —, possibly an open invitation meant for Kendrick Lamar, whose 2015 album *To Pimp a Butterfly* was an acknowledged model for the sound Bowie wanted for ★.[a] Reports that Kanye West almost immediately announced himself as Bowie's torchbearer via Twitter were greatly exaggerated, perhaps an opportunistic Yeezy backlash that reflects the shadow side of Bowie's blue-eyed-soul appeal.
   a Though if Bowie has an alter-ego legacy, let it be mutable as he was, and more so. Let anyone wear the mantle of gender-abstract changeling — *turn to face the strange* — with or without guitar.
11 Here with apologies: We all die, some sooner than others. The videos present a death rite and a temporary resurrection, a visiting wraith, respectively. Again, cf. Fred Moten: "the phantasm that the mechanical reproduction of the silenced voice emits" (118).
12 An inch higher on that page is a declaration of poetics that serves as a *Trouble Songs* credo: *be critical and sing*.
13 though a poem by that title could be found at the journal *Lana Turner*'s web site

its consolation was yet a promise.[14] Nor was its maker likely to thumb her nose, hand us her bejeweled skull, and return to her wardrobe, only to reappear with rags binding her eyes, blind buttons winking over the top,[15] as in Bowie's final, looping testaments.

In the days after Wright's and Bowie's deaths, for those who mourn the poet and rock star with the particular, half-guilty displeasure of those who know them only by their works, a number that now includes us all, they dance together into the cabinet. Those left at the station will get there soon enough.

Meanwhile, we refrain,[16] with the last book of poetry we do have: *the year in which this particular round / of troubles began.*[17]

---

14 Almost secretly available at the time (compared to the elaborate promotion for ★), however, was a new book of poetics, *The Poet, the Lion, Talking Pictures, El Farolito, a Wedding in St. Roch, the Big Box Store, the Warp in the Mirror, Spring, Midnights, Fire & All*, released like Bowie's album the previous week. A companion volume to *Cooling Time,* which mixed poetics in prose with line-broken poems in clear homage to William Carlos Williams's *Spring and All*, Wright's new prose work borrows also from sequencing techniques she used in poetry books and encouraged in the work of her Literary Arts students at Brown University. For example, her introduction to the 2011 facsimile edition of *Spring and All* is broken into multiple sections, as is a reflection on her friend and Brown colleague Robert Creeley, and an essay first published online in 2011 at *The Volta* (aka *Evening Will Come*), "In a Word, a World."[a] Those sections are each given a page, and the essays are interspersed among the volume, so we are in effect reading all of them at once, if we read the book from front to back.
   a This latter essay is notable not only for its excellence, but for the way its multi-page online layout anticipated Wright's formal, modular sequencing technique in the 2016 poetics volume.
15 Bowie's final character, Button Eyes, visually captivating if not as smartly attired in language as The Thin White Duke. David Jones, rest in peace.
16 Fred Moten: "Sometimes you are afraid to listen to the voice of the dead, to its palpable, material sound" (117). Wright's full recorded performance of *Deepstep Come Shining* from July 16, 1999 (posted at PennSound) is an achievement of voice and breath equal to the written text.
17 *One With Others* (2010), 14. Poet and teacher Carolyn D. Wright, rest in peace.

Nobody Here but We in Trouble

One/Two/Three/Four, or BIRTH/LIFE/DEATH/RESURRECTION, as Kurt Stenzel has it on his score for *Jodorowsky's Dune*,[18] which is to say the soundtrack for the film about the troubled '70s production of Alejandro Jodorowky's filmic adaptation of Frank Herbert's novel *Dune*.

Troubled, which is to say not completed, and later visited by David Lynch's troubled[19] 1984 version, which exists on celluloid.

Stenzel's album a retro-synth curiosity fully formed, in formal contradistinction to his subject, or the subject of his subject (or milieu). Album scheme in the grain of classic themed sides, from the generic/common this side/that side[20] to the iconic SILVER SIDE/BLACK SIDE.[21]

---

18 written over and presumably into the music — etched onto each side and scheduled on the back of the album
19 as in hot mess, critical nadir, and perhaps hidden gem wrapped in gaud
20 signified on De La Soul's *Stakes Is High* (1996) as a-side/a-notha side, A SIDE / ANOTHER SIDE on R.E.M.'s *Fables of the Reconstruction* (1985)
21 As inscribed on Public Enemy's *It Takes a Nation of Millions to Hold Us Back* (1988), honoring the group's legit and unofficial affiliation with the National Football League team the Los Angeles Raiders, a tip of the cap to its renegade image. The former-and-later Oakland Raiders were an L.A. franchise from 1982–94, during which time the organization's reputation for assembling troubled players was very much a part of its Just Win, Baby ethos. In 2010, former N.W.A. MC Ice Cube directed a documentary for ESPN's *30 for 30* series called "Straight Outta L.A." that explored the influence of Raiders ethos and iconography on hip-hop culture, in relation to the impact of the team's move from Oakland to Los Angeles. As of this writing, after having failed to arrange a return to Los Angeles, Raider ownership (currently, reptilian Al Davis bowl-cut scion Mark Davis) is publicly contemplating a move to Las Vegas. Whether or not this fades into a PR blip, it is worth recalling for anyone who finds the whims of the Davis clan, and the larger cultural implications of the Raiders franchise, worth considering, even as the notion of a Las Vegas Raiders team conjures Elvis Presley (or Lady Gaga dressed as Elvis) in a sequined Raiders-themed jumpsuit, singing a medley of "Bring the Noise," "Express Yourself," and "Are You Ready for Some Football?"

How any four-sided thing might adopt the self-same scheme: BIRTH/LIFE/DEATH/RESURRECTION.

Just as any concept album is captive to its own pretense — a plot and a procession, a bunch of tracks.

We are all born, and we all rise, we live and die, not necessarily in that order. So the album can't demand we listen in sequential sides (if its tracks are more fixed). And many show us as much, skipping mention on their labels, drawing eyes to sidelong run-off grooves.

A Whole House

> *There's gonna be some trouble / A whole house will need rebuilding*
> — Morrissey

The trouble promised in the first line of "Now My Heart Is Full,"[22] which opens side one, arrives in the first cut on side two, "Why Don't You Find out for Yourself." The word "trouble" has flown the coup, but the feeling remains, *sick down to my heart / well that's just the way it goes.*

No more named, trouble skims the sorry lake of the album, *a brick in the small of the back again,* as moaned by the Krazy Kat intoning "I Am Hated for Loving." By the time it comes to rest near "Speedway" at the end of the album, the rumors are true: *I never said they were completely ungrounded.*

A step aside from Destroyer's *Trouble in Dreams,* which obviates "trouble" while saturating the singer/listener,[23] Morrissey's opening salvo makes a promise it does and does not keep. If you know you're in trouble you no longer need the signs.

---

22 and the first line of Morrissey's 1994 album *Vauxhall and I*
23 That is, "trouble" sticks to the title and does not appear by name in the songs, but look here, we're soaking in it.

Nobody Knows (Great Things to Small)

The lyric floating[24] over this manuscript, from Amiri Baraka's[25] *Wise, Why's, Y's* (1995):

Wise I
>WHY'S *(Nobody Knows The*
>*Trouble I Seen)*
>*Trad.*

If you ever find
yourself, some where
lost and surrounded
by enemies
who won't let you
speak in your own language
who destroy your statues
& instruments, who ban
your omm bomm ba boom
then you are in trouble
deep trouble
they ban your
oom boom ba boom
you in deep deep
trouble

humph!

---

24 yet to sting, or stung and numbed
25 Baraka appeared in Part One as LeRoi Jones, the name under which he published *Blues People* among other works, before changing his name to Imamu Amiri Baraka in 1968. As Fred Moten says in a footnote to *In the Break,* "The question of the name is unavoidable" (271). Moten decides to use the name Baraka even when referring to work published under the name Jones, because Moten's interest is in a prolonged period of radical transition for the poet, and in honor of the super-chronological, far-reaching implications of Baraka's transformation.

probably take you several hundred years
to get
out!

We may be privileged with a sideline seat to such trouble, a ticket with a curse, but check the Jumbotron: We are here.[26]

†††

During a media presser leading up to Super Bowl XLVIII (2014), Seattle Seahawks cornerback (and Stanford University graduate) Richard Sherman was asked about being called a "thug" after a post-game braggadocio-fueled rant following a team victory in the previous week's NFC Championship game. He interpreted the question not as another opportunity to apologize for unchecked (if contrived) bravado and rhetorical showmanship, but rather an opportunity to unpack the coded language of sportscasters, radio callers and bloggers alike:

> The only reason it bothers me is because it seems like it's the accepted way of calling somebody the n-word nowadays. Everybody else said the n-word, and then they said "thug," and they're like aw, that's fine. And that's where it kind of takes me aback, and it's kind of disappointing because they know. What's the definition of a thug, really? Can a guy on a football field just talking to people — maybe I'm talking loudly and doing something, you know, talking like I'm not supposed to. … I know some "thugs," and they know I'm the furthest thing from a thug. I've fought that my whole life, just coming from where I'm coming from. Just because you hear Compton, you hear Watts, you hear cities like that, you just think "thug, he's a gangster, he's this, that, and the other," and then you hear Stanford, and they're like, "oh man, that doesn't even make sense, that's an oxymoron." You fight it for so long, and to

---

26 How do we talk about a poem that's perfect and doesn't need us? Let us pass over and return (stylus digging groove), and flip the side.

have it come back up and people start to use it again, it's frustrating.[27]

†††

During a media presser leading up to Super Bowl L[28] (2016), Carolina Panthers quarterback (and Auburn University graduate) Cam Newton was asked about widespread criticism of his on-field enthusiasm.[29]

> I think this is a trick question. Because if I answer it truthfully … but I'm gonna say it anyway: I don't think people have seen what I am or what I'm trying to do. … I've said it since day one. I'm an African-American quarterback that may scare a lot of people because they haven't seen nothing that they can compare me to.[30]

†††

---

27 "Richard Sherman Thug is another way of saying the 'n' word." *YouTube* transcript ours. Accessed February 4, 2016.
28 The game was advertised as Super Bowl 50 because the traditional Roman numeral designation does not fit the standardized Super Bowl logo template, according to Jaime Weston, the NFL's vice president for brand and creative. So says Wikipedia (so even Weston's ludicrous title is provisionally ratified). L is also the typical indication of loss on a score sheet, and since one team must technically win the Super Bowl (even if they don't get to take it home), perhaps there are other reasons, particularly in the season of Donald Trump as so-called legitimate Republican presidential candidate,[a] for avoiding an L in Super Bowl 50.
   a And hello from the flip side after the election, when we have some serious fucking trouble.
29 The question was "Why do you think that you're judged, why do you think that you've become more of a lightning rod than other athletes?" Newton has been criticized in some quarters for showboating during and after plays, as in his spectacular, frequent, and lofty (though rather un-quarterback-like) entrances into the end zone, followed by his uniform rendition of hip-hop's dabbin' dance.
30 "Cam Newton: When You Win, That Gives Them Something Else to Talk About | Super Bowl | NFL." *Youtube* transcript ours. Accessed February 4, 2016.

During a media presser leading up to Super Bowl XXII (1988), Washington Redskins[31] quarterback (and Grambling State graduate) Doug Williams was asked about his experience as a Black quarterback. The question reportedly[32] began, "Doug, obviously you've been a Black quarterback your whole life." Williams responded to the effect (in-pre-internet matters of sports media, we often rely on hearsay) that he'd been playing quarterback since high school and had always been Black. He too remembers the essential form of the question he was asked: *How long have you been a Black quarterback?*

†††

Are these Trouble Songs transcribed? Baraka has certainly signified the poetics of trouble, with its deep deep echo of erased song. Sherman, Newton and Williams, though, are they trouble singers? As in so many Trouble Songs, where something comes over the singer, and the microphone opens a void, these players, after and before the game, bear our witness. Among all the rehearsed and recycled lines, the thoughtless refrains, they find a moment to look the crowd in its recording eyes,[33] to briefly sing of what ails us: our own smallness, our failures of imagination, our withdrawal from the commons.

†††

---

31 As of this writing, Washington's professional football team is still represented by a racial slur. The irony of Washington's ignominious moniker juxtaposed with its groundbreaking Black quarterback is lost on no one who isn't lost.

32 per *Rocky Mountain News* reporter Bob Kravitz, who later claimed to have been sitting next to the reporter in question (details of this account come from Snopes.com, which investigated the following popular claim: "Before Super Bowl XXII in 1988, a reporter asked Washington Redskins quarterback Doug Williams, 'How long have you been a Black quarterback?'")

33 *We're talking about practice,* reigning National Basketball Association MVP Allen Iverson repeated many times with an incredulous array of inflections during a 2002 press conference in which he was taken to task for his imperfect record of game-prep attendance.

Trouble sings the singer, trouble (through its troubler) sings the song. Trouble sings to us even when it isn't there.[34]

†††

Then there is the game itself. Super Bowl L (2016, Santa Clara) will be remembered as another W for Beyoncé at the big game. Previously she had performed the National Anthem at Super Bowl XXXVIII (2004, Houston), and the halftime show at Super Bowl XLVII (2013, New Orleans), during which she was later credited for shutting the whole thing down.[35]

Super Bowl L was a forgettable game even if it had a storybook ending for aging white quarterback Peyton ("The Sheriff") Manning[36] at the expense of ascendant Black superstar Cam ("Superman") Newton (who muttered deflated monosyllabic replies at

---

34 or when it's dismissed by its own name, which is not the same as dismissed by name, though it is that too
35 Following her halftime show, less than two minutes into the third quarter, power went out in the Superdome, causing a 34-minute delay in the game. Baltimore Ravens linebacker Ray Lewis later suggested the outage was no accident, because it halted his team's momentum (they had a 28–6 lead), allowing the San Francisco 49ers[a] to regroup and mount an ultimately unsuccessful comeback attempt, in any case helping broadcast ratings. Others suggested (employing the loaded oxymoron "partial blackout") that Beyoncé's powerful halftime show overloaded the grid.
   a Whose quarterback, Colin Kaepernick, three years later would stir trouble from the bench (to which he had been demoted) by refusing to stand for the pre-game National Anthem, in solidarity with Black Lives Matter. Soon he joined the company of Tim Tebow as a polarizing backup QB with the best-selling jersey in the league. He found more trouble after he announced that he did not vote in the November 2016 election. By the 2017–18 season, Kaepernick was blackballed by team owners and executives, but his principled stand against police brutality continued to reverberate through the league.
36 who had a lackluster game for a historically underwhelming Super Bowl-winning Denver Broncos offense that was carried by its shutdown defense, though Manning's poor showing did nothing to discourage a stale chorus of "Victorious Sheriff Rides off into the Sunset" headlines

his post-game presser, ultimately and somewhat abruptly walking off into the darkness at the edge of the set).

Beyoncé's performance once again dominated. Co-headliners Coldplay and Bruno Mars were reduced to props, while her dance crew was elevated and politically charged, outfitted in Black Power getups[37] and organized in (Malcolm) X formation.[38]

The stage for Beyoncé's halftime performance of "Formation" was set by the previous day's release of the song's new single and video versions, which established a rich backdrop of imagery related to the Black Lives Matter anti-police brutality movement, the structurally racist government (non-)response to Hurricane Katrina (highlighting its lingering effects while radically remixing Bayou social codes),[39] and a matrix of Black Southern culture references and gleefully knowing materialist contradic-

---

37 while Beyoncé sported a gold X-emblazoned bandolier jacket designed in militant-bling homage to the one Michael Jackson wore during his 1993 world tour

38 For once in *Trouble Songs*, a footnote is a mere footnote: Predictable (but no less troubling) Fox News backlash included erstwhile NYC mayor Rudy Giuliani denouncing the performance as shamefully incendiary and anti-cop ("It was really outrageous that she used it as a platform to attack police officers"), calling for "decent, wholesome entertainment" at future halftime extravaganzas during the Super Bowl's annual celebration of America's commercial values.

39 Jeff Chang's *We Gon' Be Alright* (2016) concludes with a critical meditation on Beyoncé's album-length film *Lemonade* (which itself concludes with "Formation"). He folds in half-time staging and film location, so the site becomes one of intimate and public powerlessness:
We see her crying as she lies on the floor of the New Orleans Superdome. … She has returned to the same place where she once short-circuited her Super Bowl half-time Show, where eight years before, tens of thousands displaced by Hurricane Katrina, denigrated by the media, and treated as animals by federal and local authorities, sought refuge and comfort" (163).
Troubling the water, Christina Sharpe (*In the Wake*, 2016) recalls "the Black displaced of Hurricane Katrina held in deplorable conditions in the Superdome, [who] continue to be in a holding pattern" (72) and live in the wake of "a past that is not past, a past that is with us still" (62).

tions, all cast under the spell[40] of what *Daily Show* "Senior Beyoncé Correspondent" Jessica Williams celebrated (in a report with all the fierce allusive delirium[41] summoned by its subject) the day after Super Bowl Sunday: "The Black girl magic in that video was out of control."

---

40 just one side effect of which transforms a military exercise into OK *ladies now let's get information*
41 The highlight was a dexterous call-out of Giuliani's cynical appeal to wholesome middle-American concerns via a subtle critique of his subliminal association of "decent" with whiteness, and, in the context of his rebuke of Beyoncé's performance, the association of Blackness with indecency: "You know what's right in the middle of America? Ferguson, Missouri."

Catch a Fire: One Thing for Another

We don't need no more trouble ("No More Trouble," Bob Marley and The Wailers, 1973) — enough is enough.[42] Here again (but one year prior), as with Gil Scott-Heron's "Lady Day and John Coltrane," there's a semantic economy (and a surplus) of "trouble" to *wash your troubles, your troubles, your troubles away.* The catch is the hook, caught in the throat, on fire, eternal return. More "trouble," less trouble. Trouble called out, though its mark[43] remains.

---

42 and more, as *Catch a Fire,* the album on which the song appears as the penultimate track, marks the major label debut for the band, and a watershed moment for reggae music — so the song's eponymous line is a statement and a protection spell, a share and a shield

43 and its sign

By Any Other Name ("Trouble, Heartaches & Sadness")

How do we get from *and* to *&*? Ann Peebles's *Straight from the Heart* (1971) begins "Slipped, Tripped and Fell in Love," and rolls right into "Trouble, Heartaches & Sadness." Once the fall begins, there's no end of leaves[44] piled on.

This could be a simple matter of authorship,[45] as George Jackson wrote the first track while Peebles shares a credit with Don Bryant on the second. Or the ligature could be a bind, just as heartache & sadness are the broken couple[46] who will never split.

I knew from the very beginning / What you had in mind.

So the album begins at an ending that takes it from the top, having fallen to the bottom ("Slipped, Tripped and Fell in Love"). Lust follows clear mistake, *But I ain't worried about it.*

Then trouble is called by name, *Old Man Trouble, stop knocking at my door.* And your friends Heartache[47] (rattling the window) and Sadness (troubling the mind) are welcome here no more. But Mr. Trouble *used to be a good friend of mine.* There may be new love to ease that mind, or love may no longer take the form of Trouble with a capital T. But we hear Peebles sing, and her

---

44 & leaving
45 To the extent authorship is ever a simple matter, which is probably the extent to which any love affair is a simple matter. Like the most self-possessed musicians, Peebles possesses and is possessed by everything she sings. *I take what I want,* she sings on the final song, credited to Isaac Hayes, Mabon "Teenie" Hodges, and David Porter, after teasing, *Come and pick me up / Carry me away / ... / I'm just a little bad girl.* Her 'come on take me' come on gives (a)way to her initial boast: *I take what I want / And baby I want you.* The song, the lover, and trouble follow.
46 Their copula need not be a verb, because they do what they are (heartache aches, sadness saddens, and sadness aches) and they *are* together, indivisible.
47 another revision from the sleeve text (Heartaches gone solo), this time within rather than between song(s)

song doesn't sound quite like what she's saying — at least not the part about love easing the mind. Anyway, if she's telling us all this, we've perhaps taken Old Man Trouble's place as her good friend. We may be no better for her, since we wouldn't want to change her tune, though it clearly costs her dearly to sing it.

As on much of the album, Peebles's voice is set back a step or two in the mix. The horns don't blare, but they're assertive enough. The groove is sturdy, but again not huge.[48] It's closer to daybreak than midnight on this album, even if the party is still going — and even if the only guests are the singer, Trouble, Heartache(s) & Sadness. It's a bit of a blur, but no less sweet for that.

The album cover is perfect. Peebles stands a step or two behind the mic, head tilted slightly back, mouth just open, eyes almost (if not) closed, hands clasped at the base of her spine, body curved like a bow — both slack and taut. She is not wailing. She could be at the beginning or end of a phrase, or she could be between phrases. If she's singing, her voice is in her chest or forehead. According to the album title, it comes from the former.

Aside from "I Pity the Fool," the third to last song of the set — which comes in a raspy, pissed off wail — Peebles sounds like she looks on the cover. She looks determined but tired. She looks lean but weary. As she sings in the penultimate song, she's *99 pounds of soul*. Likewise, her voice is both embodied and beyond the body. It comes from the heart but escapes through the head. On the cover, her body is emptied of that voice, if not its soul.

---

48 Compare Peebles's version of "I Take What I Want" with Aretha Franklin's and encounter a different song. Franklin's version is all swagger and bombast (with dramatic separation in the mix), all push and no pullback. She also has backup (vocals). In contrast, Peebles's caginess is all nuance and blend. Franklin's version is another strong number on *Aretha Now* (1968), and Peebles's version is a *closer* — the final word.

Notes

> *The note is overmuch, over-abundant, over-exposed, the inexactly mirroring transparency in the dark that shimmers as the not-seen: what is made visible does not help us to see but encourages a kind of sightless empathy we need and cannot access and cannot not seek.*
> — Jen Hofer, "Proximate Shadowing: Translation as Radical Transparency and Excess"

Trouble Songs is translation and accompaniment. It is a record, both sides now.[49] That is, if we can imagine side B as subtext to side A, where subtext is becoming text. Or (/then) *Trouble Songs* is a cassette tape played on a 4-track machine from which we can hear both sides, and the other side (which is always side B)[50] plays in reverse, filling especially every A-side pause.

Footnotes make themselves visible while making the body (in)visible. Endnotes are the afterworld, to (and from) which we return. Notes access what cannot be accessed, what we can(not) hear. Trouble Songs are the conversations we have with ourselves as we listen, which accrue on subsequent listens. Those subsequent hearings arrive too soon, echo back to us as we wave them forward.

This has already been written.

To listen (and to sing) is to aspire to empathy — to share breath — and thereby achieve it. To sing (and to listen) is to embody language. To play is to vibrate, to make waves.

The dark that shimmers below the music, the record on the table, the not-seen music spinning. So with reading *Trouble Songs* and not hearing, or hearing the not-heard.

---

49 per page
50 Or see/hear (again) De La Soul's *Stakes Is High,* where there's a-side, a-notha side, etc.

A mirror through which we see.

A mirror through which we hear.

†††

> The poem makes its own kind of sense, its own kind of senselessness. The poem doesn't need the notes. The poem needs nothing. The notes need the poem. The translation needs both the poem and the notes. Or insofar as the translation is its own poem, it needs nothing. The notes come directly from and into the translation process itself — they are not afterthought or afterword, but interruption, excess, interjection, extraneous needful commentaries...
> — Jen Hofer, "Proximate Shadowing: Translation as Radical Transparency and Excess"

Here the poem is the song, one of many which play at once, as a song is in the world once and henceforth, occurring once ever, released into the world.

It is obscene, David Thomas has said, *to record a live concert. It is a performance for those who are there.*[51]

You cannot play a song twice. So says Richard Meltzer.[52]

Both statements are true/false statements.

David Thomas has made, in a sense, obscene recordings, music (with his band Pere Ubu) played for a sound engineer. And he is correct that a live recording is a monstrosity, a false thing.[53]

---

51 This is the song of memory, from a talk Thomas gave at The New School (introduced by Greil Marcus), December 2, 2009.
52 Again, the source is memory. Here let us acknowledge the hauntological influence of Meltzer's *The Aesthetics of Rock* (first published in 1970) on *Trouble Songs*.
53 acknowledged and accentuated in post-production, sometimes including overdubs and amplified or inserted applause (see Johnny Cash, Jimi Hen-

And this is in praise of false things.

Richard Meltzer describes a song that is not a song, but a performance.[54]

And yet it is true that a song ends before it is replayed. One cannot rehearse a performance.

With apologies and respect to Jen Hofer: A record makes its own kind of sound. The song doesn't need the notes. The song needs nothing. The notes need the song. *Trouble Songs* needs the song and the notes, the body and the record, and the notes are the body's song. Insofar as *Trouble Songs* needs nothing but songs. The notes come directly from and into the process of listening — they are afterthought and afterward, interruption, obscenity, excess, nonlinear interjection, extraneous unnecessary commentaries…

---

drix, James Brown, Lou Reed, Neil Young, Björk, et al.); then there's the live studio recording, the fake live recording, the knowing faux live song, etc.

54 On a related trip, even if the scenery is different, Richard Crawford in *America's Musical Life: A History* (2001) stressed "performance rather than composition as a starting point" (from the volume's Introduction).

The Author Role

Writing and reading are not the same. Reading is faster.[55] Reading that is writing (all reading) complicates the matter without resolving it. As we read our writing, we multiply.

And still we imagine the writer knows everything we do not — thinks every thought on page, in sequence, with full access to the range.

And here is where the book lies as the song lies. The singer speaks in lyric, a falsework. The song's revision is not a mastery of the past, or a setting right, but a story about its own telling. *You are here,* it sings, lying to our faces. *I am here,* it sings, one foot out the door.

A book written over a number of years, and a song sung after the singer dies. Those who passed over the book and those who passed after the book. A book among headstones. A book of crosses. One book in another. One song singing another song.

The reader overhearing. The reader singing the song.[56]

---

[55] except as a whole — the reading that precedes, accompanies and follows writing

[56] The song listening.

The Champ[57]

> *I ain't got no trouble with them Vietcong.*
> — Muhammad Ali, as quoted by Wesley Morris, "From a Blockbuster Fighter To a Country's Conscience,"[58]

There's trouble and there's "trouble" &c. This sounds familiar but so does everything. Today a terrible thing happened. One person was responsible.[59] That's how easy it is to be a ghoul.[60] That's why we're so scared. Some of us are already gone.[61]

---

57 Thanks to Ray DeJesús for SMS sparring in preparation for this Trouble Song.
58 Ali has also been quoted, "I ain't got no quarrel with them Viet Cong" (e.g. BBC, *The New York Times, Wired*), "I ain't got no quarrel with those Vietcong" (e.g., History.com), "I ain't got no quarrel with the Vietcong" (e.g. *The Daily Telegraph*), "I got nothing against no Viet Cong" (e.g. *Fusion*). It is unclear whether variations are attributable to the transcriptions of reporters and editors or to various instances of Ali's pronouncement, or some of each.
59 A floating refrain that is provable as true and false. As the days pass and this cruel summer reveals new horrors — more unarmed Black Americans shot by police officers, more lone gunmen channeling broad frustrations, more reportage conflating positions, intentions and affiliations, more politicians seeking dubious solutions — we find it ever more difficult (one month after writing the sentence that carries this note) to sing the song of individual responsibility.
60 On June 12, 2016, a man shot up a nightclub, it seems, because he could not stand the thought of two men dancing. He claimed to be a Muslim. If Ali were alive he would tell us the truth: No Muslim would do such a thing. After the September 11, 2001 terrorist attack on NYC, Ali was quoted in a *Reader's Digest* interview: "I am angry that the world sees a certain group of Islam followers who caused this destruction, but they are not real Muslims" (as cited in Tim Stanley's June 4, 2016 Opinion piece for *The Telegraph*, "Muhammad Ali was an American idol and a Muslim. Read his words on Islam"). Stanley also quotes a statement Ali made in December 2015 ("Presidential Candidates Proposing to Ban Muslim Immigration to the United States"): "I believe that our political leaders should use their position to bring understanding about the religion of Islam and clarify that these misguided murderers have perverted people's views on what Islam really is."
61 Ali claims, in conversation with David Remnick (as reported in Remnick's *King of the World*), that he was scared one time, before the first round of his first title fight with Sonny Liston, and we believe him. Or: Fear is a form

We do not know how to properly crawl into the larval state. One friend broke his collar and crawled below the front stair to heal, or die. Another disappeared into himself. Three others died swerving to avoid an animal crossing their path. How many die fleeing their ostensible protectors? There is no end to early death.[62] Nor to crawling.

Trouble's undersong: *I have come from the land of myth and blame. All the latter is upon me for good reason; the former is death's grin. I have seen the world lying in its grave. The grave is empty, just bones.*

†††

In the famous photo from Ali-Liston II (1965), Ali says everything but what he says, even when the caption says what he says. *Get up. Get up and fight.* Ali knows the fix is in. Ali still does not know if he beat the odds the previous year, when Liston did not answer the bell. Listen, this is not to say Sonny Liston should not have lost to Cassius Clay or Muhammad Ali. He lost to both, though he threw the latter fight.[63]

Get up and fight, Ali says. This is not a moment of triumph, but of disillusionment. The image, one angle, one version, hangs

---

of trouble, and Ali was a troublemaker in the ring as well as out of it, and death is the threshold for both fear and trouble. Near the other end of his career, after his third fight with Joe Frazier — the Thrilla in Manila, October 1, 1975 — Ali claimed the brutal fight was the closest he had come to death.

62 In vain we resist turning the book into the book of the dead, as every book becomes the book of the dead. And every book is written while death takes its due, so that some are alive and dead over the course of the book, and the book carries those deaths, or is haunted by them.

63 "And me and trouble was never far apart" (50), Reminck quotes Liston about his boyhood. And he carried the title like trouble; no other bearing was allowed to him.

above the President's desk.[64] Triumphalist Metanarrative vs. Death of the Dream: Meta by a knockout.

Ali in 1965 is learning America. He has found the key he does not want. Liston lays down, one eye on the floor. This[65] is not a love song.[66] This is not the key to victory. This is the beginning of a whole lot of trouble.

---

64 That it is a less famous version of that moment — Obama has a black-and-white print of John Rooney's photo, rather than the more celebrated color shot by Neil Leifer — suggests an alternate and coincident history. Rooney caught two iconic images from that moment: one that is similar to Leifer's image, but from one seat over in black-and-white, and the one Obama favors, in which Ali is not swiping left. Some of the apparent disdain is gone from the latter, but it loses none of its ambiguity. Which suggests the possibility that Obama knows the difference between what the photo says and what it shows.
65 This photo, this storied moment, and this Trouble Song, all of which dance around the ring (and ring around the rosie).
66 Nor is it an attempt to speak for the dead, even if these photos (and songs) speak to us.

Dear Trouble[67]

Kristin Hersh sings to trouble. There is no cover.

There is a room between singing trouble and singing to trouble. There is a summoning, a spell and counter-curse: to sing trouble under the guise of influence.[68] And there is a lullaby beseeching trouble to lie still, go easy.[69] Singing to trouble, Hersh lets it come close, knows it's already in her heart. Her song[70] is not a speech act, but an acknowledgement.

The song's placement at the middle of the track list for *Sunny Border Blue* (2001) cannot be arbitrary. Covers often go early or late in an album, but this is not a cover, it's a bedfellow. A cryptmate. Tucked in, shielded.

Trouble, oh trouble set me free.

What does the face of trouble look like? *Death's disguise hanging on me?* That face that covers death. The one that curdles in the mirror.[71]

In that room between singing trouble and singing to trouble is the song. No one agrees which song it is, and no one cares who sang it first.

---

67 Thanks to Keala Ramos for direction.
68 as though trouble can hear, and will listen
69 knowing well trouble is in attendance
70 Cat Stevens renounced it, though he only ever had "Trouble." Hersh takes the song where it has never been, gives it trouble, makes it ache. Even the treacly see/me and wine/mine rhymes can't take the edge off Hersh's delivery.
71 Edith Scob as Christiane checks her new face after her father, Dr. Génessier, encourages her to "smile… not too much" in Georges Franju's *Eyes Without a Face* (1960).

The End of Trouble

If trouble is inevitable as death is inevitable, if death is the only release from trouble, and if we wish to be free from trouble, why not end it all?

But this would be to make life a problem with a solution. Trouble has no solution, as death is not a solution to life, but an end to it.

In *Notes on Suicide,* Simon Critchley considers the possibility, via downbeat philosopher E.M. Cioran, that suicide is an optimistic act committed by optimists who can no longer function in the world as optimists. In *The Trouble With Being Born,* via Critchley, Cioran advises those who come to him with suicidal intentions, "What's your rush? You can kill yourself any time" (quoted in Critchley, 72–73).

And here's the crux (and precipice) for troubled singer/listeners: *This song is the end.* And there's the paradox of the Trouble Song. It's the end that stops ending, and starts again. The last song is the song before, forever until the last song we hear, or sing.

You can kill yourself any time. The Trouble Song puts off all kinds of death, by inviting all kinds of trouble.[72] Refrain: *Life may run out on us, but we have time for one last song.* The dead hear no more songs, though they sing. So the singer/listener becomes the twice disembodied singer — once by memory or recording, once by separation of body and spirit. Those of us who remain in the flesh sing and listen to deaf ghosts. Our troubles are not the same though we share the song, which has come all this way, through time and space, through myth and blame, to deliver us.

---

72 Trouble, after all, is not another word for death, even as death is the ultimate trouble.

Song[73]

The first time Brigit Pegeen Kelly intones *sweet* in her best-known poem, "Song," it describes a sound. A girl listens to the train's horn passing each night, until the night she doesn't hear the horn, and knows her goat is dead.

Another song, the song that opens the poem, replaces the horn that will someday announce the girl's train out of this town where the boys who killed her goat and hung its head in a tree still hear that song. It is the song the goat's head sings to them.

> Listen: there was a goat's head hanging by ropes in a tree.
> All night it hung there and sang. And those who heard it
> Felt a hurt in their hearts and thought they were hearing
> The song of a night bird. …

What they hear is the poem, or what we hear is the goat song. It is a song of death that sings to the living, all those who live in the murdered world. This song has two refrains. One describes the boys' labor to remove the goat's head: *It was harder work than they had imagined.*[74] Another concludes the poem, the credo of this Trouble Song, and the final words we need to hear again:

> Not a cruel song, no, no, not cruel at all. This song
> Is sweet. It is sweet. The heart dies of this sweetness.

---

73 For Brigit Pegeen Kelly (1951–2016)
74 Once it occurs at the end of a line, and once it is cut after *they*, the last words *Had imagined* singing back at them from the next line.

Last Call

The lights go on in Club Trouble. Time to face the day. Facing our compatriots through the country of the night is another matter. All implore the barkeep: *One more round, and then maybe one more.* She's no more anxious for the light than we are.

Down the lights go, back to a level that allows our countrypeople's eyes to reopen, if not gain their focus. A few more songs, then. Someone approaches the jukebox, one of the last in town that doesn't have a search bar.

Every book ends or is thrown down in disgust. Some books never end because we don't bother to finish them. Here's how this one turns toward the door and waves over its back.

†††

The Log Lady's[75] kindred gesture: She defers telling the trouble she has seen, and instead shows us her log.[76] Her trouble song goes *Someday*[77] *my log will tell you what it saw that night.* Verse after verse excised from the broadcast and added to the record.[78]

---

75 She does not come from the mind of David Lynch, not anymore, though she is the only one who truly belongs in *Twin Peaks,* standing as she does at the edge (that is to say, the center) of town.
76 which must recall every trouble the town has produced
77 Or was it *Some of these days...*?
78 The Log Lady monologues that open each episode with cranky prophetic poetry were not part of the show's 1990–1991 network run, but are available in retrospect. In the versions we have seen, they look dubbed on VHS from some spectral broadcast directly from the TVs of Twin Peaks, an interruption of *Invitation to Love,* the soap opera that plays on loop in the fictional town. In fact, the Log Lady intros were created for the 1993 syndicated run of the show on Bravo. They are the footnotes placed before the body. Another integral lapse occurs in 2015–2016, when the band Xiu Xiu recreate and extend Lynch and Angelo Badalamenti's soundtrack with *Plays the Music of Twin Peaks.* The set was first commissioned by Australia's Gallery of Modern Art for "David Lynch: Between Two Worlds," a celebration of the show's 25th anniversary. *I'll see you in the trees,* Xiu Xiu's Jamie Stewart moans. He

†††

I'm sorry, I'm nervous, she interrupted the song. Who could blame her? Patti Smith stood in the middle of a balcony over the stage, surrounded by an austere army of musicians. Below her were arrayed dignitaries and other titled people in royal finery. She was singing on behalf of Bob Dylan, who had to wash his hair. She was singing the longest song, with its endless lyrics about the hard rain that was gonna fall 50 years ago.[79] She sang it over flood waters. More than once, the song lost her in the current.

Greil Marcus writes about the moment when a band finds a song during performance, and about the moments when the song happens around them, or fails to happen. At the Nobel Prize award ceremony, December 11, 2016, in troubled times, Smith bore witness to "Hard Rain's A-Gonna Fall" — the absence of the song and its singer. Its refusal *to wash your troubles, your troubles, your troubles away.*

†††

> Waves of anger and fear
> Circulate over the bright
> And darkened lands of the earth,
> Obsessing our private lives;
> The unmentionable odour of death

So writes W. H. Auden in "September 1, 1939," which Lou Reed loops into "Waves of Fear," from 1982's *The Blue Mask,* an al-

---

becomes the voice that calls Laura Palmer to the darkness at the edge (that is, the center) of town. *I just know I'm going to get lost in those woods again tonight,* we hear her recorded voice say at the end of the first episode.[a]

a which follows the pilot and reboots the show, or recasts it as a death-driven loop, a hauntology

79 having forgotten the moral of "Rainy Day Women #12 & 35": when they ask if you want to get stoned, tell them you're good

bum that opens with a tribute to the poet (and Reed's former teacher, departed some 16 years prior, in the impossibly distant '60s) Delmore Schwartz. *Waves of fear, pulsing with death* gasps Reed, over that unmentionable odour, an abjection that makes the words go round.

Those to whom evil is done / Do evil in return, sings Auden. This is a Trouble Song, one of many. Trouble is not evil, but it comes around.

> Faces along the bar
> Cling to their average day:
> The lights must never go out,
> The music must always play,
> All the conventions conspire
> To make this fort assume
> The furniture of home;
> Lest we should see where we are,
> Lost in a haunted wood,
> Children afraid of the night
> Who have never been happy or good.

Auden is cruel as that erstwhile light that must never come on. Truly we do not await its return. We are less afraid of the deep night than we are of the cold day. But yes, we seek a place of rest (until our barkeep sings the final song: *You don't have to go home, but you can't stay here*[80]). And as long as the music plays, trouble is far off where we can see it — where we can join it in the distance from our problems, which are so much worse for their illusory solutions. Trouble will kill you but it won't pretend to go away for good.

Those other and more famous lines, we leave them to the poem.

---

80 To which we reply, *It might not be such a bad idea if I never went home again.*

APPENDICES

Appendix A: Demo

Trouble on the Line

published in *Kitchen Sink*, Volume 3, Issue 2 (2005)

Troubles, no troubles, on the line, begins the second song on the Silver Jews LP, *Starlite Walker*. Actually, it's the first song on the album, if you don't include the preceding "Introduction II," which is a spoken/sung invitation to the record, a warm room with a well-stocked beer fridge. "Trains Across the Sea" opens with another intro, this time just piano, which could be called "Introduction I." Perhaps, after such stoned gestures of welcome, one should be ready for the double-speak of the song's first line.[1] Perhaps one has also merely been warned: You've entered a place where the unspeakable is spoken of, where life is a dream we're having even now. Troubles? What are those?

The Silver Jews seem built to confound. *Starlite Walker* is often listed as the band's first album, from 1994, though the Jews dropped *The Arizona Record* in 1993. The latter sounds like a living room recording made on a drunken dare. Sometimes it sounds like a joke, sometimes like a hoax. The first song, "Secret Knowledge of Backroads," sounds like wasted buddies singing along to their favorite song on the stereo. Almost ten years later, a live version by Pavement appeared as a bonus track on the deluxe reissue of *Slanted & Enchanted*. Call it a half-cover, since Pavement singer Stephen Malkmus, credited as Hazel Figurine, sang on the original recording. Pavement's version was recorded in 1992 for BBC Radio 1's John Peel Show, which means it hit the air before the original was released. It's a complete heartbreaker, with a perhaps telling Malkmus ad lib, where he sings,

---

[1] Incidentally, the line is also an echo of a country standard called "Trouble on the Line." If intentional, the reference might be a disavowal or a bit of self-deprecation by a band known to dabble in country stylings. Later, principal Silver Jew David Berman would move to Nashville, Tennessee and record a country record, *Bright Flight*. In 2004, country mama Loretta Lynn would co-write her own "Trouble on the Line."

"It's not as good as the first EP." He could be referring to Pavement's *Slay Tracks 1939–1966* (released as a 7" in 1989), the Silver Jews' *Dime Map of the Reef*, which would be released in 1993, he could be talking about *The Arizona Record*, or he could just be talking shit.

Troubles, no troubles, on the line. Don't worry about how you got here; have a seat, have a beer, sing along — whether you know the words or not.

"Trains Across the Sea" has always bothered me, not so much in the sense of "to worry or trouble," as *Webster's New World College Dictionary* first defines it, but in the second sense, "to bewilder or fluster." It's part of *Starlite Walker*'s unreadable introductory gesture, which puts me in mind of the first few lines of John Ashbery's "Self-Portrait in a Convex Mirror":

> As Parmigianino did it, the right hand
> Bigger than the head, thrust at the viewer
> And swerving easily away, as though to protect
> What it advertises. ...

What are these troubles, brought up only to be dismissed? Though the singer insists they do not exist, he has handed them to me. I began to notice "troubles" appearing in other songs, and they were usually handled with something like care.[2] I have regularly revisited these songs, and they continue to hang me up, warmly, at the door. Still, they at least invite me into their rooms. I will never know them, and so I return.

What Would the Community Think?

As we awaited the follow-up to Cat Power's devastating 1998 breakthrough album, *Moonpix*, Chan Marshall offered *The Covers Record*, which was, sure enough, a record of covers (in-

---

[2] As when a pitcher throws a curveball — he casts something away from him, though he first holds it deliberately, and he throws it with the intent to confound.

cluding a cover of one of her own songs). Some considered it a diversion, something to tide us over, or something to distract Marshall from the pressure to top *Moonpix*. It might have also been a perverse way of telling listeners that you can only do something once: Marshall reworks some of the songs to the point of unrecognizability. Her "(I Can't Get No) Satisfaction" strips the song of its calling-card guitar riff and tosses it into a pile beside her bed, along with its chorus. She makes the song her own, and if I've had a few beers, I'll tell you I prefer it to the Stones' original.

On side one, Marshall also covers an old standard, "Troubled Waters," in which she announces that "I must be one of the devil's daughters," then says, "I'm going down to the devil's daughter/ I'm gonna drown in that troubled water." She may be singing about being in over her head, but she's already proven with "Satisfaction" that she can hold her own with the devil's music.

On the second side, Marshall takes on Bob Dylan's "Paths of Victory,"[3] and after jaunty intro piano and scenery (a trail, a road, a "clearer road up yonder"), we come to the chorus, which begins, "Trails of troubles and your roads of battle," and concludes "they lead paths of victory we shall walk." Perhaps she is preparing herself for her "true" follow-up, which would come three years later in the form of *You are Free,* or YOU ARE CAT POWER FREE, as it reads on the cover, which may or may not be a fuck-you to everyone who bothered her about recording the follow-up to *Moonpix* (or accused her of stalling with a record of covers).[4]

---

[3] Dylan has recorded at least 24 songs with some form of "trouble" in the lyrics, several of them far better known than this song, which appears on Dylan's *Bootleg Series, Vols. 1-3 (Rare & Unreleased) 1961-1991.* I'm not accusing Marshall of willful obscurity — she covers "Sea of Love," too. She sings Dylan's song because it sings to her, and this sense of singing back at songs haunts the album in a way that certifies it as a Cat Power record.

[4] As a heavily anticipated follow-up, a covers record is a disappointment, but as a record of covers, *The Covers Record* is a victorious achievement.

Marshall's own troubles with performance-anxiety, her erratic concerts that can move an audience to gooseflesh and tears, then frustrate them with false starts, talk of unhappy concert hall spirits, and center-stage meltdowns, have added to Cat Power lore. Marshall has spoken about a dark night of the soul in which she was troubled by demon specters which she could only keep at bay by singing and playing her guitar. This was the night she wrote most of *Moonpix,* using her cat power to save her mind. It's this off-kilter self-assurance that gives her a grip on the old, troubled songs of *The Covers Record.*

Good and Gone in Song

A few cymbal taps, a commotion of voices in a room, and Jason Lytle croons "Trouble with a capital T," as Grandaddy launches "Lost on Your Merry Way." His voice, as usual, is a sweet, warm falsetto with a hint of irony. He's probably not being sarcastic, but he lets you know he might take it all back — whatever it is he's talking about, which is often unclear. As with the Silver Jews' David Berman and Stephen Malkmus, he's committed to sincere bafflement, as if he's not sure what to make of words, or doesn't quite trust them. By the second verse, Lytle's trouble line has morphed into "Trouble with people like me." In the first verse, the line is followed by "'Tie him down' they said," and now it's "Tie 'em down and then they vanish instantly." Like Chan Marshall, Lytle isn't above fucking with the listener to make a point, and here, he might as well be defending each singer's right to keep the meaning of his troubles to himself.

Appendix B: Cover

Record Related #3: And I could use a thing or two...

> Lambchop, *Mr. M* (Merge) /
> live at Le Poisson Rouge, NYC, 4/19/12
> published in *The Rumpus* (August 2, 2012)

Who put the M in *Mr. M,* and what might that M be? Maybe it has to do with the gallery of dandies on the album artwork. Three line the bottom of the front cover, two the back, and one heads a label on each side. We read, above two Van Gogh-ish portraits on the back cover (all swirling visages and lacinato backgrounds), that Kurt Wagner — house painter, guitarist and word-man for the Nashville alt-chamber indie-rock collective known as Lambchop — is responsible for these images, which come from a series called *Beautillion Militaire.* The title references an organization dedicated to providing "personal development experience and recognition ... for African-American male high school students." M as in Mr. and *Militaire.* The dandies are perfectly overdressed for the melodic melodramatics and stylized, exaggerated precision of *Mr. M.*

NPR reports that *Mr. M* was once *Major League Bummer,* and the album notes thank "Major League Baseball for their assistance with the title." In an interview for *Denver Westword,* Wagner bemoans MLB's nixing of the title *Mr. Met,* as folks might mistake the album for the New York Mets' mascot. As a concession, track four is "Mr. Met." We also read, in the lower right-hand region of the back cover, that the album is dedicated to James Victor Chesnutt, musician, who passed away in late 2009 (truly a major-league bummer).

These are among the stories that might hit us before we listen to *Mr. M.* Once we turn it on, the music takes over. Hmm, there's that M again.

The lyric micromanagement *Maybe add some flutes* places Wagner in the opening song, fiddling with the phrasing. *Grandpa's coughing* sounds like a coffin *in the kitchen.* Just so, *a ladder* becomes *the latter.* Before we know it, *Here come the crazy flutes again,* and again the flutes are only in the words of "If Not I'll Just Die." These misdirecting call-outs nonetheless make us attend the strings and piano — an ornate, if deflated, segue to the album. The mood throughout will be a sagging elation, an emotional hangover. We won't be carried all the way away, though we'll go there with the song.

"2B2" is flash fiction in slow motion. "The Good Life (*is wasted*)" is country indulgence. "Never My Love" is a billet-doux backed by "a London string ensemble." "Buttons" is Suburban Gothic. It's all supper-club Americana, all par for the many courses we've come to expect from Lambchop.

Simple as it seems, *It was good to talk to you while we're cooking / Sounds like we're making the same thing* ("2B2") manages to be an astonishing lyric. It takes us to two kitchens and hangs us up on the phone, with a precision that is in no way fussy. There's a gorgeous piano figure splitting (or joining) the lines, and the warm, doubled vocals underscore the image (two voices overlapping on the line(s)).

The music works on vibration. Each note is a duration, everything left open. Note, pulse. Sometimes Cat Stevens appears to appear to sing ("Gone Tomorrow"), as Wagner borrows Stevens's chuckling vibrato for the mid-chorus line *Looks like water flows over from somewhere else.* He pulls it off by pairing it with a familiar Wagnerian aside, speak-sung in his own voice: *And I could use a thing or two today.* The strings swoon, and the broken voice grounds us, while periodically taking us off guard, either with its own swing, its phrasing, or its vocalese punctuation adrift — *Oh… yeah.*

We forget the open spaces, but they're there, perhaps filled with lyric reflection (ours). Or we can already associate notes and vocal beats, so they become interchangeable. "Gone Tomorrow" spreads out and wades. Drifts off, comes back, ends. Sounds familiar. Maybe it's a wake. They say Vic Chesnutt haunts the album. Tours the stage toward the end of side one, which ends on an extra beat.

Notes and beats are the same, pairing and aligning to a vanishing point of distinction, a propulsion reflected in the vocal phrasing. First song, side two, "Mr. Met" brings it home. Each word on a beat, a note. Sometimes crowding two syllables on a note, but mostly monosyllabic, and when the words lengthen, they often have their own beats: scansion as diagramming sentences. Sometimes one syllable bumps along multiple notes, but not often enough to be distracting. It's background music that takes you to the background. Easy listening made complex.

A Trouble Song Interlude

"Buttons" is just over five minutes of faded suburban melodrama. It's a reverie with no sense of escape, an accumulated loss. *There's not much for you this summer* is ostensibly about work, but it seems to have a broader implication — a whole lot of *nothing, as months and weeks have passed into years / and your life has changed in some histrionic ways*. It's both mild-mannered and hysterical, as time oscillates in more and less predictable ways. We're past the surprise that so much has passed, and on to living out of time. The linearity of weeks to months is reversed: Months give way to weeks, all of which are digested by years. There were better days, the speaker says, before you ended up collecting trash beside the motorway, but then again: *I used to know your girlfriend / back when you used to have a girlfriend / she was nice and you were not / but I was the big prick back then too*. We're past nostalgia, as well. The good old days are just the old days, and instead of pining for the past, we *wonder what she thinks of when she thinks back now of you*. The distinction between now and then is that back then, we wouldn't have imagined ourselves as we are now. We no longer have that luxury, even in retrospect.

The progression from then to now was not inevitable, nor can it be changed, and that's our trouble. Or, as Wagner sings it, *Been better times for those that are in trouble / and maybe there'll be some better times for you*. The real trouble, which the song attempts to correct by dispelling nostalgia, is that things *seem bet-*

ter than they were. The song leaves it at that, and we're left with the suspicion that we can only visit the past on the path to (and from) the present. Also, there's the possibility that by the time we get to *were* at the end of the song, we have a new past, which was the present only a moment ago, so that we're no longer talking about all those years ago, but are still misremembering the way we were (just now *and* back then). Which is to say, at best, we always come back to our desire to change the course we've already run, but we at least realize our mistake. At worst, we fool ourselves into believing there was a time before trouble arrived, or before we arrived in trouble, that lonesome town.

Showtime

Kurt Wagner sings like he's going out of style. He introduces a song by suggesting we continue with the "life love death loss particularly loss thing." He shakes his guitar, shakes himself, as he plays and sings — his body is his instrument and the guitar is a pick.

Let's rewind. Upon arrival, we notice Ira Kaplan, of Hoboken's own Yo La Tengo, sitting near the merch table at the entrance to the club area. Hmm.

When the opening band, Charlie Horse, comes out, Kaplan's presence at the entrance becomes even more conspicuous. On stage are Kaplan, Georgia Hubley and James McNew, AKA Yo La Tengo. Tonight they're Charlie Horse, which covers an array of songs, mostly recent YLT numbers, in a lounge-y style suitable to the setting, as well as the headliner. Hubley's light touch, and her casual, standing brush-percussion, suggest that drumming is not about power but maybe about force. It's not quite easy listening, but it's definitely pop, in the old sense of the word. The approach is especially affecting for a sublimely relaxed take on "Sugarcube," from 1997's *I Can Feel the Heart Beating as One*, played as though it was on that album's 2000 follow-up, *And Then the Nothing Turned Itself Inside-Out*. It's just the right aperitif before the main course. Mmm, fresh Lambchop.

Delicacy is a delicate ant and a hammer. Lambchop's set opens with organ grind, or ride. After a libretto, Wagner does the only thing he can do: starts the show with the first song on *Mr. M,* which begins, *Don't know what the fuck they talk about...*

As Wagner shows over and over again, vibrato and emotion are the same thing, or cannot be distinguished, just as we recognize the piano as the sounds it makes. *I represent you,* he sings, putting mustard on it. He exaggerates his strum gesture — this is a rock band, however sedate. And *Mr. M* is Lambchop chamber pop, fully realized.

He sings like he's going out of style. The band is with him all the way. Tonight, we all follow Mr. Music: We do the life love death loss particularly loss thing.

Appendix C: Remix

Troubadours & Troublemakers:
Stirring the Network in Transmission & Anti-Transmission

originally presented at the Electronic Literature Organization 2014 conference panel "Troubadours of Information: Aesthetic Experiments in Sonification and Sound Technology," with Andrew Klobucar;[5] revised and expanded for *The Poetics of Computation, Special Issue of Humanities* (2017)

> *transport [of a message] transforms*
> — Régis Debray

> *[I]t is one of the important tasks of poems to short-circuit the transparency that words have for the signified and which is usually considered their advantage for practical uses.*
> — Rosmarie Waldrop

> *I am a DJ. I am what I play.*
> — David Bowie

Let's imagine a modern context in which a DJ figure tracks trouble town to town. She seeks a (power) system (of amplification), just as she plays for and through a system of signs and sounds. We don't have to abandon the idea of a trouble singer[6] in order

---

[5] During the conference panel presentation, the essay was projected behind the speaker, who was accompanied by clips from referenced songs. Each prose block was laid out in landscape view, counterbalanced by associated footnotes. This setup was intended to acknowledge and engage multiple nodes and modes of audience attention, while suggesting a verse-chorus or call-and-response form to the text. Notes were read selectively, and improvised.

[6] The trouble singer is a figure who sings "trouble" in place of "actual" trouble, thus temporarily dispelling the latter and allowing the audience to commune over this exorcism while sharing a sense of their burdens. The Trouble Song summons trouble in an aestheticized form that not only shields the audience (temporarily) from its worries, but protects the singer from a

to introduce this figure: Our Mixmaster (aka MC) is the trouble singer in another era, with other tools.[7]

Furthermore, let's triangulate the DJ[8] and the trouble singer with a third figure: the troubadour. We should have reference, recall and recourse to all three (plus) figures while at once imagining them as non-exclusive.[9] We seek a trouble singer who may be DJ and troubadour, while we recognize the usefulness of making connections and distinctions between these figures.

We listen for (and sing) connections between lyrics and music, while acknowledging that song does not absolutely or neces-

---

potentially debilitating candor (or public exposure). Meanwhile, the Trouble Song functions as a screen onto which the audience (and the singer) may project their own troubles.

7   We may conflate DJ, Mixmaster and MC, while allowing each term to add layers to our key figure, the trouble singer. (We adopt terminology from the *Trouble Songs* project, where Trouble Song is a proper noun but trouble singer is not, though the latter usage may appear inconsistent here with the other key figures: DJ, Mixmaster and MC. Let's say the trouble singer is a generic figure that encompasses the other more specific figures.) We think of the DJ (disc jockey) as broadcaster and collector/controller of records — or media curator. The Mixmaster moniker emphasizes technique (turntablism) and the signal/noise interface signified by the scratch. (We might further explore this path in relation to Kim Cascone's consideration of glitch music as the product of digital tools that enable the foregrounding of error and signal failure, so that audio processing tools, like the turntable, become instruments rather than media. See "The Aesthetics of Failure: 'Post-Digital' Tendencies in Contemporary Computer Music.") Meanwhile, the Mixmaster's crossfade (via multiple turntables, along with other devices including laptop and CD console) takes us across media and directs transmission flows between sources. The MC (mic controller) is the rapper or maker of toasts, whose verbal dexterity and feel for the audience serve to monitor and inflect communal affect. We will toggle between these terms to emphasize various roles and skills embodied by our contemporary trouble singer, even while the DJ may combine these roles (as the DJ needs the Mixmaster's technological skills and the MC's genius). Meanwhile, these footnotes will tend to sing a more formal song than the body text, as a more explicit academic backup, or a hybrid (re)mix of *Trouble Songs* tones, or a straight cover of the same song, a simulcast transmission. Pardon the mixed (troubled?) metaphor.

8   in her multiple guises

9   As with the media operated by the Mixmaster, they are a confluence of signals.

sarily distinguish between the two: Sung (and/or rapped) words become music,[10] and instruments (be they lyres or synthesizers) speak to us. Over-adherence to formal and technical distinctions brings its own troubles (among them genre trouble, but also a tendency to miss the song while listening to the device), and our objective remains to locate trouble in and around song.

Since we investigate via language, let's look within language for clues, cues and affinities. We begin with "troubadour" and "trouble," in order to imagine the trouble singer as a (modern) troubadour. Along the way, we might re-discover a connection (or a mix, to bring the DJ to the party) between singing and making: The trouble singer has a reputation not only as summoner and evoker of trouble, but as troublemaker and troubler.[11] Music travels, songs make their rounds, and the troubadour both follows them and leads them from context to context, scene to scene: the troubadour attends.[12] This may be to confuse the singer for the song, but language and song are full of such confusions, conflations and slippages.[13] They might even be composed of them.[14] The songbook of trouble (were there such thing) might itself be a compilation of these confusions.

---

10 just as poem becomes song
11 Here we might add that the troubadour's reputation for knowledge of technique and form evokes the technical (and technological) prowess of the Mixmaster, just as the troubadour's vocality recalls (or preforms) the MC's mic skills.
12 Further along the road, we note the country blues tradition of itinerant musicians after emancipation — as discussed by Leroi Jones in *Blues People*, and Angela Y. Davis in *Blues Legacies and Black Feminism* — and the ways these ambulatory cultural practices abet the floating folk lyric, where recognizable phrases hop from song to song and place to place (see also Greil Marcus, "The Old, Weird America" and Luc Sante, "The Invention of the Blues"). This line of thinking is elaborated in *Trouble Songs: A Musicological Poetics*.
13 Consider the DJ's bag of records, many of which carry the signal of the MC, whose song travels with or without her. Still, the DJ may toast (to sample a term from the origins of hip-hop, at the emergence of the MC's distinct role) over the top of that signal, spinning a new verse over the spinning record(s).
14 Rather than confuse singer for song, we might (remixing Cascone) conflate singer and song with device, and device with the failure of the device. We

If Trouble Songs travel in a pre-20th century mode,[15] they are carried place to place by individuals and in migrant cultural practices. The trouble singer performs a social function in bringing "trouble" to town, then taking trouble away.[16] This economy of trouble follows the lineage of the troubadour, a figure from the High Middle Ages who amplifies love and stirs volatile emotions. *The Oxford English Dictionary* traces the etymology of troubadour via the troublesome (and questionable)[17] verb form "from Latin turbāre to disturb, through the sense 'turn up'" and suggests a comparison with "the form French troubler." Perhaps, then, we can imagine the troubadour as a carrier of trouble: a troublemaker.[18] Less contested etymology suggests the troubadour finds, invents or composes his song.[19] That the troubadour is known (and remembered) for love songs puts him on trouble(d) ground, just as the trouble singer seems preoccupied with the vicissitudes of love (as rivaled only by her attention to death — and of course love and death are seldom strangers, not for long and certainly not forever).

---

might then amplify the glitch: synechdochal failure, or device failure as device, or failure for device. The device, too (like or as the song), might carry us (temporarily) away from trouble — or replace one trouble with another. Glitch can be transformative or transporting, but it also signals imminent crash.

15 That is, if we bracket (or delay) for a moment the advent of electromagnetic wave transmission, which will extend and further complicate song travel.

16 Again we go back (and forward) to early-20th-century country blues and folk lyric mobility and transfer. This is worth mentioning again because itinerant blues may be considered in the context of this essay as a reference point connecting the troubadour to our contemporary DJ figure — where allusion, floating lyric and sample wax transhistorical.

17 Indeed, the etymological commentary opens, "The origin of the verb itself is questioned."

18 Whether this figure might also either be a troubleshooter, or might seem to require troubleshooting, remains to be seen.

19 Here the etymological connection between troubadour and the medieval Latin *tropus,* via trope (again per OED) connects with verse, which suggests a sense-making prosodic arrangement we might also think of as version, mix or flow. This related sense of trope as verse phrase also evokes a (call and) response as introduced in the medieval Western Church and carried through MC flow.

The troubadour relates songs of love, and the trouble singer presents a "trouble" lyric to which her audience can relate.[20] Trouble and love pass through both songs, and both singers. Both figures are trusted and blamed with (and for) carrying their charge. They are artists, servants and provocateurs — and here let us recall that the provocateur is a troublemaker for hire. She stirs trouble, foments sentiment, disturbs and turns up discourse. The troubadour and trouble singer can certainly dig it, as they perform their services, for whatever coin.

The DJ is also a digger (of crates, beats, tropes[21]). Whatever she turns up is amplified. Have beats, will travel; have system, will supply power for amplification. Such power calls this version of the trouble singer like a block party DJ to a hackable streetlamp. The moth flies by night and makes a light show of her pursuit. The DJ brings a flock to the light of her mixing board.[22] Turns it on — pumps up the volume on her amplifier.

Troubadour, trouble singer and DJ are all seekers of the song that finds us where we live:[23] love, trouble, the beat of our hearts (in and out of our accustomed rhythms). All bring their cargo, their information, their music, from elsewhere, and take something from us as they move along.[24] We are thankful, skeptical

---

20 The successful Trouble Song lyric balances pathos and detail with a generic sense of inclusiveness and discretion, which protects singer/listener privacy while allowing for communal feeling and commiseration.

21 which she turns, literally, a remix of trope's etymology from Greek *tropos*, 'turn'

22 making use of the MC's geniality and the Mixmaster's technique, which are no sweat (see here Erik B. & Rakim's foundational hip-hop album *Don't Sweat the Technique*)

23 The song finds us by ear and by eye. The DJ sees what she plays, from cover to groove, while the Mixmaster sees sounds as wave forms to be manipulated, amplified, numerically sampled, patterned as information. Meanwhile, at least in retrospect, we all see trouble coming.

24 Allow us to reintroduce the troubadour, who models a form of cultural remix, where historical traditions are de-contextualized, then re-contextualized in the mix for contemporaneous situations and loci. Much is brought to the transhistorical party, including more trouble: a provisional order is established with a wink, set up to be knocked down as the revelry gets underway.

and aroused. In trouble, as in song, we are bereaved, bereft, at a loss, and full of gain. *I ain't seen nothing but trouble /... / And I go to the place where good feeling awaits me / ... / Oh, and I go crazy when I can't find it* sings Marvin Gaye in "Flyin' High (In the Friendly Sky)," deep in and far above his own troubles, and ours.[25]

***

As Robert Casillo has it,[26] "[M]etonymy is defined as the substitution of the container for the contained" (142). So "trouble" as a linguistic container promises, in the Trouble Song, to dispel trouble. This is not the way language is supposed to work; rather, it's the way language works. The trouble singer makes slippage work for her.

***

"[T]he troubadour poem is supplementary, an attempt to overcome absence, difference, and delay" (Casillo 139). Whereas the trouble singer attempts to amplify the absence, difference and delay of trouble with the application of "trouble," the troubadour seeks to prolong the unconsummated heart-on, presenting poem as fetish for the lady (or object of desire in the trouba-

---

25 As we'll see (and can hear for ourselves), *What's Going On* (1971), from which this cut comes, is full of trouble. A year later, Gaye graces the album cover of the soundtrack to *Trouble Man,* above a spliced action shot of the lead film actor (the composition shaped in a T for Trouble with a capital T, while the O in trouble and the A in Marvin are shot through with extra holes). He sings its title song and adds vocal textures to a few other numbers, but the album is mostly instrumental and incidental accompaniment to the Blaxploitation film by the same name. This is a whole other world of (representational) trouble, outside the scope of this essay, though in terms of *Trouble Songs*' musicological poetics, we might say the Trouble Man character Gaye doubles for on the soundtrack plays the part for those who want a taste of trouble without paying for their meal: "Trouble" in place of trouble, as *Trouble Songs* has it, and as explored above (or below) in a moment.

26 in "Troubadour Love and Usury in Ezra Pound's Writings"

dour's song). But if, as Casillo goes on to suggest, the troubadour makes his living[27] by forestalling consummation (his own and others'), he has something in common with the trouble singer, who sings trouble away with "trouble." (Here is the transmission of anti-transmission, where the audience gets exactly what it bargains for.)[28] For his part, the troubadour sings love (intercourse) away with "love" (the language of desire in song).

***

A syllogism, of sorts:

troubadour — song — lady; trouble singer — song — trouble

This is a formal and relational comparison, with song at its fulcrum: all terms are not equivalent. The lady is not trouble, despite what the boys might say. But the object of the troubadour's song confers with the object of the trouble singer's song. The troubadour claims to draw the lady closer, while pushing her (tantalizingly) away,[29] and the trouble singer calls "trouble" to put trouble at bay.[30] To stir up, then forestall, remains a powerful linguistic gesture, in any medium, with any toolset. "Trouble"? What trouble?

***

Let's add our third figure to the mix:

---

27 or gets around
28 And let's recall the Mixmaster's crossfader, which re-places or conflates one song/signal for another, and makes possible the potentially infinite dilation of the break (as we'll see).
29 And yuck, etc. This heteronormative and sexist display is ripe, of course, for drag dressing-up-as-dressing-down via torch song.
30 a refrain, to refrain: She has no intention of calling trouble itself, except to call it "trouble" — to re-place trouble (elsewhere, anywhere but here)

troubadour — song — lady;   trouble   singer — song — trouble;
DJ — track — beat

The DJ is one who DJs — as Mixmaster, the one who drops (and turns/tropes) the beat. The mode of transmission remains the song (or track[s]).[31] As ever, the song is mix and remix, informed and composed of cultural material. Like our first two figures, the DJ/Mixmaster stirs up and forestalls: finds the hook,[32] loops it into her beat, and lets it spin. Here we call to mic the MC, who might ride the beat and let "trouble" flow. We might also consider the breakbeat, for which the Mixmaster finds and loops a drum pattern[33] to literally forestall a climax in her track. This may be accomplished via turntables and crossfader or with a digital sampler and sequencer.

***

"The transmission, or the transport of information in time, is to be distinguished radically from that of communication, or the transport of information in space, even if they combine in reality," writes Régis Debray, in "What is Mediology?" (as translated by Martin Irvine). We might consider *the transport of information in time* as a description of song, and in the case of the Trouble Song, what follows is true: We may radically distinguish this transport of "trouble" from communication of trouble. As for the transport of information in space, whether or not it is distinguished from communication, the trouble singer complicates or even frustrates such transmission, by design. Consider

---

31 city to city, beat to beat
32 Here we find Wikipedia's entry for hook to be of use (recognizing also the suitability of this source, as cultural and linguistic sample and remix): musical idea or short riff.
33 Archetypal breakbeats come from James Brown's "Funky Drummer" or The Incredible Bongo Band's "Apache," as mixed on two turntables by DJ Kool Herc (circa early '70s in The Bronx), as he cut between two copies of the same record to extend the drum break for the benefit of the b-boys and b-girls on the dance floor.

again the floating lyric — that is, tropes borrowed and re-turned (or re-tuned) by the singer. *Troubles, troubles, I've had them all my days; trouble in mind; trouble on the line; leave your troubles behind; nothing but trouble.*[34] These tropes turn up *here* having come from *elsewhere,* but we've heard them before and can't be sure they crossed a line from there to here. Or we know the lines are crossed, but can't be sure if these bits of information transmitted here to there or there to here, or if they were and are always here and there, a circuit lit up.[35] Debray again: "[T]he origin is what arises at the end." Process does not necessarily imply procession from a point of origin.[36] The song was always here and always there,[37] but the trouble singer performs the magic of transport in which "trouble" arrives to take (or keep) trouble away, and we too are transported: to and from trouble, via song. And still: Every Trouble Song sings to (and from) the others. Thus "trouble" is transmitted, and trouble is transmuted.

***

"The object of transmission does not preexist the mechanism of its transmission" (Debray once more). We necessarily (and correctly) confuse the figure —: troubadour, trouble singer, DJ — for the message —: love, trouble, beat. Each is associated with a technique and a technology;[38] nor can we any longer distinguish the analog from the digital. The DJ's media were record and turntable, and now include the laptop[39] — all of which re-

---

34 see also Appendix A: "Trouble Will Find You" in this volume.
35 or, again, two turntables linked by crossfader
36 Nor does the troubadour arrive (though he attends the song) — always out of place, the troubadour (like the Mixmaster et al.) is stuck in a loop of here/there. Just so, the trouble singer rides the break (sic) of trouble/"trouble."
37 And here we can further illustrate and complicate the matter with reference to electromagnetic radio waves and wireless communication, where source and signal translocate and exist in multiple and proliferant destinations, and the nature, form and format of the source is transmogrified.
38 where (in this verse) technique is delivery, and device (be it metaphor, guitar or computer) is technology
39 the medium *and* the tool/instrument

quire, as does the DJ, a system of amplification, and an audience to receive the transmission (or anti-transmission, in the case of the Trouble Song).

***

Marvin Gaye sings into the intercom, "Flyin' High (In the Friendly Sky)" *without ever leaving the ground.* From his view, he sees *nothing but trouble,* and spins this trope, his for the song, a floating lyric transmitted to us, hung over the precipice of good feeling and self-destruction. Gaye's voice, above the strings, vibes and rhythm, carries us where the singer can't go. *Nobody really understands,* he sings, sparing us. Gaye announces, in the liner notes for the 1971 album *What's Going On,* "[Y]ou shouldn't have to pay any special attention to the lyric on 'Flyin' High In the Friendly Sky' just because I think you ought to."[40] End transmission.

---

40 It's up to you, of course. If you do keep the song spinning, and listen through Gaye's delivery to the words, which are perfectly clear even as they soar above signification, you'll hear a cocaine blues, probably, but you'll also hear a love song, and a song of brotherhood. You'll also hear, in the last, circling verse, *the boy who makes slaves out of men* to whom the song — and the singer — is hooked. You might also notice the way the previous song, "What's Happening Brother," lands on the opening vocal oohs of "Flyin' High," making the connection between the returning soldier and the troubled mind. *Can't find no work, can't find no job my friend* sings the soldier in "What's Happening Brother," and the grounded pilot answers *In the morning, I'll be alright, my friend,* before correcting himself later in "Flyin' High": *Well I know I'm hooked, my friend.* He knows well the answer to the soldier's final question, *What's been shakin' up and down the line* (and the soldier knows he knows — just like the album title, his question has no question mark): *Without ever leaving the ground / ... I ain't seen nothing but trouble baby.*

Works Cited

Ashbery, John. "The Other Tradition." *Houseboat Days*. New York: Penguin Books, 1977. 3. Print.
Ashbery, John. "Self-Portrait in a Convex Mirror." *Self-Portrait in a Convex Mirror*. New York: Penguin Books, 1975. 68. Print.
Baraka, Amiri. "Wise 1." *Wise, Why's, Y's*. Chicago: Third World Press, 1995. Print.
Bergvall, Caroline. "Middling English." *Meddle English*. Callicoon: Nightboat Books, 2011. 5-19. Print.
Bernstein, Charles. "Artifice of Absorption." *A Poetics*. Cambridge: Harvard UP, 1992. Print.
"big black - kerosene." *YouTube*. Web. 6 Apr. 2013. https://www.youtube.com/watch?v=ZLr5EXyoQCE.
Bob Marley and The Wailers. "No More Trouble." *Catch a Fire*. Tuff Gong/Island Records, 2009 [original release 1973]. LP.
Bowie, David. ★. Columbia Records, 2016. LP.
Bowie, David. "Blue Jean." *Tonight*. Virgin, 1984. MP3.
Boggs, Dock. "Country Blues." *Anthology of American Folk Music Vol. 3*. Ed. Harry Smith. Doxy, 2009. LP.
Butler, Judith. "Subjects of Sex/Gender/Desire." *Gender Trouble: Feminism and the Subversion of Identity*. New York: Routledge, 1990. 1–34. Print.
"Cam Newton: When You Win, That Gives Them Something Else to Talk About | Super Bowl | NFL." *YouTube*. 4 Feb. 2016. https://www.youtube.com/watch?v=wgf8bgfcqN8.
Cascone, Kim. "The Aesthetics of Failure: 'Post-Digital' Tendencies in Contemporary Computer Music." *Audio Culture: Readings in Modern Music*. Ed. Christoph Cox and Daniel Warner. Continuum: New York, 2004. 392–399.

Casillo, Robert. "Troubadour Love and Usury in Ezra Pound's Writings." *Texas Studies in Literature and Language* 27.2, Twentieth-Century Literature (1985): 125–53. JSTOR. Web.
Cat Power. *The Covers Record*. Matador, 2000. LP.
Chandler, Raymond. *The Big Sleep*. New York: Vintage Crime, 1992. Print.
Chang, Jeff. *We Gon' Be Alright*. New York: Picador, 2016. 158–168. Print.
Clover, Joshua. *Their Ambiguity*. Quemadura, 2003. Chapbook, CD.
Clover, Joshua. *the totality for kids*. Berkeley: U of California P, 2006. 55. Print.
Coates, Ta-Nehisi. "Nina Simone's Face." *The Atlantic*, 15 March 2016. Web. theatlantic.com/entertainment/archive/2016/03/nina-simone-face/472107/
Critchley, Simon. *Notes on Suicide*. London: Fitzcarraldo Editions, 2015. Print.
Davis, Angela Y. *Blues Legacies and Black Feminism*. New York: Pantheon, 1998. Print.
Debray, Régis. "What Is Mediology?" Trans. Martin Irvine. *Le Monde Diplomatique*, August 1999, 32. Georgetown University. Web. http://faculty.georgetown.edu/irvinem/theory/Debray-What_is_Mediology.html.
Destroyer. *Trouble in Dreams*. Merge, 2008. LP.
Dylan, Bob. *Shadows in the Night*. Columbia Records, 2015. LP.
Foster, Hal. "Against Pluralism." *Recodings: Art, Spectacle, Cultural Politics*. Port Townsend: Bay Press, 1985. 13–32. Print.
Fox, Aaron A. *Real Country: Music and Language in Working-Class Culture*. North Carolina: Duke UP, 2004. Print.
Gaye, Marvin. *Trouble Man*, Tamla, 1972. LP.
Gaye, Marvin. *What's Going On*, Tamla, 1971. LP.
Grandaddy. "Lost on Yer Merry Way." *Sumday*. V2 Records, 2003. LP.
Hazlewood, Lee. *Trouble Is a Lonesome Town*. Smells Like Records, 1999 [original release 1963]. LP.
Hirsh, Kristin. "Trouble." *Sunny Border Blue*. 4AD, 2001. Web.

Hofer, Jen. "Proximate Shadowing: Translation as Radical Transparency and Excess." *Harriet*, 30 April 2016. Web. http://www.mdpi.com/2076-0787/6/2/21/htm.

Johnson, Jeff T. "Troubadours & Troublemakers: Stirring the Network in Transmission & Anti-Transmission." *The Poetics of Computation, Special Issue of Humanities*. Eds. Andrew Klobucar and Burt Kimmelman. 2017. Web.

Johnson, Robert. "Me and the Devil Blues." *The Complete Recordings: The Centennial Collection*. Columbia, 2011. CD.

Jones, LeRoi. *Blues People: The Negro Experience in White America and the Music That Developed From It*. New York: Morrow Quill Paperbacks, 1963. Print.

Lispector, Clarice. *The Passion According to G.H.* Trans. Ronald W. Sousa. Minneapolis: U of Minnesota P, 1988. Print.

Lim, Dennis. *The Man From Another Place*. Boston: Houghton Mifflin Harcourt, 2015. Print.

Lynch, David, dir. *Eraserhead*. Libra Films International, 1977. Film.

Mancini, Donato. *Loitersack*. Vancouver, BC: New Star Books, 2014. Print.

Marcus, Greil. *The History of Rock 'n' Roll in Ten Songs*. New Haven: Yale UP, 2014. Print.

Marcus, Greil. *Invisible Republic: Bob Dylan's Basement Tapes*. New York: Henry Holt, 1997. Print.

Morris, Wesley. "From a Blockbuster Fighter to a Country's Conscience." *New York Times*, 5 June 2016.

Morrissey. *Vauxhall and I*. Sire/Rhino, 2013 [original release 1993]. LP.

Moten, Fred. *In the Break: The Aesthetics of the Black Radical Tradition*. Minneapolis: U of Minnesota P, 2003. Print.

Moure, Erín. "The Public Relation: Redefining Citizenship By Poetic Means." *My Beloved Wager*. Edmonton, Alberta: NeWest P, 2009. 163–171. Print.

The National. "All the Wine," "Mr. November." *Alligator*. 4AD, 2007. LP.

The National. *Trouble Will Find Me*. 4AD, 2013. LP.

Nelson, Willie. *The Troublemaker*. Columbia Records, 1976. LP.

Newsom, Joanna. "Good Intentions Paving Company." *Have One on Me.* Drag City, 2010. LP.

Peebles, Ann. *I Can't Stand the Rain.* Fat Possum Records, 2009 [original release 1974]. LP.

Peebles, Ann. *Straight From the Heart.* Hi Records/Fat Possum Records, 2015 [original release 1972]. LP.

Retallack, Joan. ":RE:THINKING:LITERARY:FEMINISM: (three essays onto shaky grounds)." *The Poethical Wager.* Berkeley: U of California P, 2003. 110–144. Print.

Reed, Lou. "See That My Grave Is Kept Clean." *The Harry Smith Project: Anthology of American Folk Music Revisited.* Shout! Factory, 2006. CD.

Remnick, David. *King of the World.* New York: Random House, 1998. Print.

Renck, Johan (Director). "★" [music video]. 2015. *YouTube.*

Renck, Johan (Director). "Lazarus" [music video]. 2016. *YouTube.*

"Richard Sherman Thug is another way of saying the 'n' word." *Youtube.* Web. 4 Feb. 2016. http://www.youtube.com/watch?v=wPSiOCC8nvc.

Ryzik, Melena. "Carefully Calibrated for Protest." *New York Times,* 26 Aug. 2012.

"ST. VINCENT COVERS BIG BLACK at BOWERY BALLROOM NYC May 22, 2011." *YouTube.* Web. 6 Apr. 2013. http://www.youtube.com/watch?v=fVhCo7PoVpA

Sante, Luc. "The Invention of the Blues." *Kill All Your Darlings: Pieces 1990–2005.* Portland: Verse Chorus Press, 2007. 177–206. Print.

Scott-Heron, Gil. "Lady Day and John Coltrane," "Home Is Where the Hatred Is." *Pieces of a Man.* Flying Dutchman, 1971. LP.

Sharpe, Christina. *In the Wake.* Durham: Duke UP, 2016. Print.

Silver Jews. "Trains Across the Sea." *Starlite Walker.* Drag City, 1994. LP.

Simone, Nina. "I Put a Spell on You." *I Put a Spell on You.* Philips Records, 1965. Web.

Smith, Bessie. "Downhearted Blues." *Bessie Smith: The World's Greatest Blues Singer.* Columbia, 1970. LP.

Smith, Harry, ed. *Anthology of American Folk Music.* Smithsonian Folkways Recordings, 1952. LP.

Sontag, Susan. *Against Interpretation.* New York: Picador, 2001. Print.

Stanley, Tim. "Muhammad Ali was an American idol and a Muslim. Read his words on Islam." The Telegraph, 4 June 2016. Web. http://www.telegraph.co.uk/opinion/2016/06/04/muhammad-ali-was-an-american-idol-and-a-muslim-read-his-words-on/.

Tosches, Nick. "Screamin' Jay Hawkins: Horror and the Foot-Shaped Ashtray." *Unsung Heroes of Rock 'n' Roll.* Cambridge: Da Capo Press, 1999. 155–164. Print.

Toufic, Jalal. *Vampires: An Uneasy Essay on the Undead in Films.* Sausalito, CA: Post-Apollo, 2003. Print.

Waldrop, Rosmarie. "Alarms & Excursions." *The Politics of Poetic Form: Poetry and Public Policy.* Ed. Charles Bernstein. New York, NY: ROOF, 1990. Print.

Williams, William Carlos. *Spring and All.* New York: New Directions Pub., 2011. Print.

Wilson, Carl. "Why I Hate the National." *Slate,* 28 May 2013. Web. http://www.slate.com/articles/arts/music_box/2013/05/the_national_s_trouble_will_find_me_reviewed_too_many_crescendos.html.

Wright, C.D. *Cooling Time: An American Poetry Vigil.* Port Townsend: Copper Canyon Press, 2005. 61. Print.

Wright, C.D. *Deepstep Come Shining. PennSound,* 16 July 1999. Web. media.sas.upenn.edu/pennsound/authors/Wright-CD/Port-Townsend_1999/Wright-CD_Deepstep-Come-Shining_Copper-Canyon-Session_Port-Townsend-WA_7-16-99.mp3.

Wright, C.D. *One With Others.* Port Townsend: Copper Canyon Press, 2010. 14. Print.

Wright, C. D. *ShallCross.* Port Townsend: Copper Canyon Press, 2016. Print.

Index of Names

Albini, Steve 94
Anderson, Sini 28
Ashbery, John 39–40, 160
Asleep at the Wheel 69
Auden, W. H. 154–55
Badalamenti, Angelo 153
Baraka, Amiri (see LeRoi Jones) 35–37, 51, 133, 136, 170
Barthes, Roland 33, 66, 85
Barth, John 78
Bejar, Dan 55–57, 132
Benning, Sadie 28
Bergvall, Caroline 19, 91
Berman, David 47, 159–60, 162
Berninger, Matt 96–99
Bernstein, Charles 103
Beyoncé 137–39
Big Black 94–95
Bikini Kill 28
Björk 56, 145
Bloom, Harold 33
Bob Marley and The Wailers 140
Boggs, Dock 17–18, 42
Bowie, David 50–51, 118, 125, 127–29, 168
Bratmobile 28
Bryant, Don 141
Buscemi, Steve 119
Burch, Thora 119
Butler, Judith 22, 29, 33

Byrne, David 88
Callahan, Bill 45–46, 55
The Carter Family 112–13
Cash, Johnny 45–46, 48, 69–70, 144
Cascone, Kim 169–70
Casillo, Robert 173–74
Cat Power (see Chan Marshall) 32, 42, 51–52, 55, 61, 70, 89, 160–62
Chandler, Raymond 20
Chang, Jeff 138
Clark, Annie 94–95
Clover, Joshua 40
Coates, Ta-Nehisi 122
Coltrane, John 47, 140
Conrad, CA 126
Costa, Gal 78–79
Crawford, Richard 145
Critchley, Simon 151
Dalton, Karen 42, 51
Davis, Angela Y. 35–36, 38, 170
Debray, Régis 168, 175–76
De La Soul 130, 143
Destroyer (see Dan Bejar) 55–57, 132
Dylan, Bob 32, 63, 69, 70, 107, 116–17, 154, 161
Erik B. & Rakim 172
Fateman, Johanna 28
The Feelies 119
Foster, Hal 38, 49
Fox, Aaron A. 30–31
Franju, Georges 150
Franklin, Aretha 142
Gacy, John Wayne Jr. 73–74
Gaye, Marvin 18, 112, 173, 177
Ginsberg, Allen 33
González, José 109
Grandaddy 29, 162
Hanna, Kathleen 28

Hawkins, Screamin' Jay 121–22
Hazlewood, Lee 48
Hejinian, Lyn 40
Hell, Richard 112
Hirsh, Kristin 53, 150
Hofer, Jen 143–45
Holiday, Billie 35, 47, 117
Hopper, Jessica 74
Hubley, Georgia 166
Jackson, George 141
James, Skip 119
Jefferson, Blind Lemon 17, 107–8, 116
Johnson, Jeffrey T. 89
Johnson, Robert 107, 120, 126
Jones, LeRoi (see Amiri Baraka) 35–37, 51, 133, 136, 170
Jones, Richard M. 69
Julie Ruin 28
Kaepernick, Colin 137
Kaplan, Ira 166
Kelly, Brigit Pegeen 152
Kristeva, Julia 33, 71
Lamar, Kendrick 128
Lambchop 163–67
Lang, Fritz 73
Lefebvre, Henri 120
Lethem, Jonathan 88
Le Tigre 28
Lim, Dennis 23–24
Lispector, Clarice 26
Liston, Sonny 147–49
Lynn, Loretta 24, 159
Lynch, David 23–24, 95, 130, 153
Lytle, Jason 29, 30, 162
Malkmus, Stephen 159–60, 162
Marcus, Greil 17, 42, 45, 82, 95, 118–20, 123, 144, 154, 170
Marshall, Chan 32, 42, 51–52, 55, 61, 70, 89, 160–62
McNew, James 166

Meltzer, Richard 144–45
MEN 28
Ali, Muhammad 147–49
Morrissey 113, 132
Moten, Fred 33, 127–29, 133
Moure, Erín 180
The National 96–99
Nelson, Willie 21, 29, 64
Neuman, Molly 28
Newsom, Joanna 54, 63, 112
Newton, Cam 135–37
Nine Inch Nails 45
Olsen, Angel 111
Pavement 159–60
Peebles, Ann 32, 93, 141–42
Pere Ubu 144
Public Enemy 91, 130
Rainey, Ma 35
Reed, Lou 17, 108, 112, 145, 154–55
Remnick, David 147
Renck, Johan 124
Retallack, Joan 22
Samson, JD 28
Sante, Luc 37, 42–45, 170
Sartre, Jean-Paul 67, 70
Schwartz, Delmore 55
Scott-Heron, Gil 32, 45–47, 67, 107, 127, 140
Sharpe, Christina 138
Sherman, Richard 134–36
Silver Jews 47, 159–60, 162
Simone, Nina 70, 121–22
Sinatra, Frank 116, 117
Smith, Bessie 19, 35, 43
Smith, Harry 17, 81–84, 108
Smith, Mark E. 96
Smith, Patti 154
Smog 32, 45–46, 55

Sontag, Susan 76
Spector, Phil 64
St. Vincent (Annie Clark) 94–95
The Staple Singers 113, 116
Stein, Gertrude 37
Stenzel, Kurt 130–31
Stevens, Sufjan 73–75
Stewart, Jamie 153
Stroffolino, Chris 85
Talking Heads 88
Thomas, Dave 144
Thunders, Johnny 68
Tosches, Nick 121
Toufic, Jalal 96, 99
Vail, Tobi 28
Veloso, Caetano 78–79
Waldrop, Rosmarie 106, 168
Waters, Muddy 32
Whitman, Walt 126
Williamson, Sonny Boy 84
Williams, C.K. 40
Williams, Jessica 139
Williams, William Carlos 102–6, 129
Wilson, Carl 98
Winehouse, Amy 32, 64, 119
Wolfe, Allison 28
Wright, C.D. 103, 123, 128–29
Xiu Xiu 153
Yo La Tengo 166
Young, Kevin 36
Young, Neil 62, 69, 145
Zolf, Rachel 33

Index of Titles

"★" 127–29
★ 128–29
"2B2" 164
"99 Pounds" 142
"The Aesthetics of Failure: 'Post-Digital' Tendencies in Contemporary Computer Music" 169
The Aesthetics of Rock 144
After the Gold Rush 69
Against Interpretation 76
"Against Pluralism" 38, 49
"Alarms & Excursions" 106
"All the Wine" 97
Alligator 97
American IV: The Man Comes Around 45
America's Musical Life: A History 145
Anthology of American Folk Music 17, 81–84, 108
The Anxiety of Influence 33
A Poetics 103
Aretha Now 142
A River Ain't Too Much to Love 45
The Arizona Record 159–60
"Artifice of Absorption" 103
"A Stop at Willoughby" 48
Back to Black 64–65
"Bay of Pigs" 56
Bay of Pigs 56
Better Call Saul 115
"big black — kerosene" 94–95

The Big Sleep 20
Bikini Kill 28
"Blank Generation" 112
"Blue Jean" 50–51
The Blue Mask 154
Blues People: The Negro Experience in White America and the Music That Developed From It 35–37, 133, 170
Blues Legacies and Black Feminism 35–36, 38, 170
Blue Velvet 24
Bootleg Series, Vols. 1–3 (Rare & Unreleased) 1961–1991 32, 161
Buffy the Vampire Slayer 115
Burn Your Fire for No Witness 111
"Buttons" 164–65
Camera Lucida 66
"Cam Newton: When You Win, That Gives Them Something Else to Talk About | Super Bowl | NFL" 135–37
"Can't Keep My Eyes on You" 68
Catch a Fire 140
The Cell 40
"Chartsengrafs" 30
City of Daughters 56
Cooling Time: An American Poetry Vigil 128–29
"Country Blues" 17, 42
The Covers Record 32, 51, 160–62
"The Darkest Day" 24
Deepstep Come Shining 129
"Devil Got My Woman" 119
"Divers" 112
Dont look back 69
Don't Sweat the Technique 172
"Downhearted Blues" 19, 43
"Down the Line" 109–10
The Downward Spiral 45
Dune 130–31
"Easy" 63
Eraserhead 23–24
Everybody's Autobiography 37

Eyes Without a Face 150
Fear of Music 88
Feminist Sweepstakes 28
The First Collection of Criticism by a Living Female Rock Critic 74
"Formation" 138–39
Frank 64
Gender Trouble: Feminism and the Subversion of Identity 22, 29
Ghost World 119
Girl Germs 28
"Gone Tomorrow" 164
The Good Earth 119
"Good Intentions Paving Company" 54
"Gotta Serve Somebody" 69
The Grey Album: On the Blackness of Blackness 36
"Hard Rain's A-Gonna Fall" 154
The Harry Smith Project: Anthology of American Folk Music Revisited 17, 108
Have One on Me 54, 63
"Heaven" 88
Here's Loretta Lynn 24
High Violet 96–97
The History of Rock 'n' Roll in Ten Songs 118–19
Hit Reset 28
"Home Is Where the Hatred Is" 47, 155
Houseboat Days 40
"Hurt" 45–46
"I Am Hated for Loving" 132
"(I Can't Get No) Satisfaction" 51, 61, 161
I Can't Stand the Rain 93
"If Not I'll Just Die" 164
Illinoise 73–75
"I'm a Fool to Want You" 117
"I'm Gonna Pack My Troubles" 24
"I'm New Here" 45–46, 127
In the Break 33, 127, 128, 129, 133
In the Wake 138

"In This Hole" 51
"Introduction II" 159
"The Invention of the Blues" 37, 42–43, 170
Invisible Republic: Bob Dylan's Basement Tapes 17, 42, 82
"I Pity the Fool" 142
"I Put a Spell on You" 121–22
I Put a Spell on You 121–22
It Takes a Nation of Millions to Hold Us Back 130
"I Take What I Want" 141–42
Jodorowsky's Dune 130–31
Kaputt 56
"Keep It to Yourself" 84
"Keep on the Sunny Side" 113
"Kerosene" 94–95
Kill All Your Darlings: Pieces 1990–2005 42
King of the World 147–48
"Kingsport Town" 51
Kitchen Sink 26, 159
Krazy Kat 132
"Lady Day and John Coltrane" 47, 140
Lady in Satin 117
"Lazarus" 128
Le Tigre 28
"Like a Hurricane" 62
Lost Highway 95
"Lost in the Paradise" 78–79
"Lost on Yer Merry Way" 29–30, 162
M 73
"The Man of METROPOLIS Steals Our Hearts" 73–75
The Man From Another Place 23–24
"Me and the Devil Blues" 107, 127
Meddle English 19
"Middling English" 19
Mr. M 163–67
"Mr. Met" 163, 165
"Mr. November" 97
Moonpix 160–62

My Beloved Wager 80
"Naked if I Want To" 51
Nausea 67, 70
"No More Trouble" 140
Notes on Suicide 151
"Now My Heart Is Full" 132
One With Others 123, 129
Orange Blossom Special 48
"The Other Tradition" 40
The Passion According to G.H. 26
"Paths of Victory" 32, 52, 161
Phases and Stages 64
Pieces of a Man 47
"Pink Rabbits" 97
Plays the Music of Twin Peaks 153
The Poethical Wager 22
The Poet, the Lion, Talking Pictures, El Farolito, a Wedding in St. Roch, the Big Box Store, the Warp in the Mirror, Spring, Midnights, Fire & All 129
"Proximate Shadowing: Translation as Radical Transparency and Excess" 143–45
"The Public Relation: Redefining Citizenship By Poetic Means" 80
The Punk Singer 28
"Rainy Day Women #12 & 35" 154
Real Country: Music and Language in Working-Class Culture 30–31
Recodings: Art, Spectacle, Cultural Politics 38, 49
"Red Apples" 51
"Rehab" 64
":RE:THINKING:LITERARY:FEMINISM: (three essays onto shaky grounds)" 22
Requiem for an Almost Lady 48
"Richard Sherman Thug is another way of saying the 'n' word" 134–36
Run Fast 28

"Screamin' Jay Hawkins: Horror and the Foot-Shaped Ashtray" 121
"See That My Grave Is Kept Clean" 17, 107–8
"Self-Portrait in a Convex Mirror" 39–40, 160
Self-Portrait in a Convex Mirror 39–40, 160
September 1, 1939" 154–55
Shadows in the Night 16–17
Six Feet Under 125
Slanted & Enchanted 159–60
"Slipped, Tripped and Fell in Love" 141
Slow Train Coming 69
"Someday Blues" 32
"Song" 73
"Speedway" 132
Spring and All 102–6, 129
"ST. VINCENT covers BIG BLACK at BOWERY BALROOM NYC May 22, 2011" 94–95
Starlite Walker 159–60
Straight From the Heart 141–42
Stakes Is High 130, 143
"Subjects of Sex/Gender/Desire" 22, 29, 33
Sumday 29, 162
"Summer Days" 63
Sunny Border Blue 150
"Sweedeedee" 51
Tar 40
Texas Gold 69
The Daily Show 139
"To Know Him Is to Love Him" 64, 119
"That Lucky Old Sun" 117
Their Ambiguity 40
"'Tis a Pity She Was a Whore" 127
the totality for kids 40
Toward an Architecture of Enjoyment 120
"Trains Across the Sea" 47, 159–60
"Troubadour Love and Usury in Ezra Pound's Writings" 173–74

"Trouble" 32, 53, 150
"Trouble, Heartaches & Sadness" 141–42
Trouble in Dreams 55–57, 132
"Trouble in Mind" 32, 61, 69–70, 121, 176
Trouble Is a Lonesome Town 48
"Troubled Waters" 51, 161
"The Troublemaker" 21, 29
The Troublemaker 21, 29
"Trouble Man" 18, 112, 173
Trouble Man 173
"Trouble No More" 32
"Trouble on the Line" 109, 159
Trouble Will Find Me 96–98
The Twilight Zone 48
Twin Peaks 153
"Unfrucktheworld" 111
Unsung Heroes of Rock 'n' Roll 121
"Valerie" 65
(Vampires): An Uneasy Essay on the Undead in Films 96
Vauxhall and I 113, 132
"Wade in the Water" 113
"Waves of Fear" 154–55
We Gon' Be Alright 138
"What Is Mediology?" 168, 175–76
What's Going On 173, 177
Where Are You? 116–17
"Why Don't You Find out for Yourself" 132
"Why I Hate the National" 98
"Why Try to Change Me Now" 117
"Will the Circle Be Unbroken" 112–13
"Wise 1" 133
Wise, Why's, Y's 133
"You Can't Put Your Arms Around a Memory" 68

Credits

Thanks to Mark Bibbins, Rachel Zolf, and Martin Beeler for comments and suggestions on an early version of this manuscript. Thanks to the *Kitchen Sink* crew for advice and audience on an even earlier version. Thanks to Jonathan Loucks for endless record sessions in another San Francisco, where I learned to talk about music. Thanks to my collaborator and co-conspirator Claire Donato, who helped me figure out what musicological poetics might look and sound like. Thanks to Stephanie Strickland, Andrew Klobucar, Azareen Van der Vliet Oloomi, Chris Stroffolino, Jake Kennedy, Kevin McPherson Eckhoff, Ray DeJesús, Matthew Choate, Danniel Schoonebeek, Anna Gurton-Wachter, MC Hyland, Ian Dreiblatt, Brenda Iijima, and everyone else who offered encouragement, song suggestions, and readership over the course of this project. Thanks to Greil Marcus for his inspiring practice of music writing as cultural listening.

Thanks to Scott Silsbe and other editors at *The New Yinzer* for publishing early excerpts. Thanks to Miranda Mellis, Tisa Bryant and Kate Schatz for including "Lost in the Paradise" in *Encyclopedia Vol. 3*. Thanks to Julia Bloch and Michael Hennessey for massive patience and care in publishing a generous helping of multi-mediated Trouble Songs at *Jacket2*.

Thanks to Eileen Joy, Vincent W.J. van Gerven Oei, and everyone at punctum books for radical hope.

Thanks to Mom and Dad for ears and early exposure to vinyl. And Kathryn, for teaching me about the smarter audience.

Here's to keeping the record spinning. Here's to leaving the book open. See you in the run-off groove.

Troubles, no troubles…

www.ingramcontent.com/pod-product-compliance
Lightning Source LLC
Chambersburg PA
CBHW072044160426
43197CB00014B/2616